Heaven-Bound Rebels
Rebels
The Bible's Study Notes on Suicide

A.D. Carroll

ISBN: 9798704329121

Cover design by EBook Launch

For WILLIAM BLAKE CARROLL,
The real author in the family

CONTENTS

1   Introduction   1

2   Part One: Those Who Have Gone Before   6

3   Abimelech (Judges 9)   10

4   Samson (Judges 16)   16

5   King Saul (1 Samuel 31)   23

6   King Saul's Armor Bearer (1 Samuel 31)   37

7   Ahithophel (2 Samuel 17)   39

8   Zimri (1 Kings 16)   43

9   Judas (Matthew 27)   48

10 Part Two: In Good Company   53

11 Moses (Exodus 2)   55

12 King David (2 Samuel 11)   59

13 Saul (Acts 22)   65

14 Part Three: A Sentiment Shared by Many   68

15 Moses (Numbers 11)   70

16 Job (Job 6)   74

17 Elijah (1 Kings 19)   82

18 Jeremiah (Jeremiah 20)   86

19 Jonah (Jonah 4)   91

20 Paul (2 Corinthians 1; Philippians 2)   96

21 Part Four: For Those Left Behind   101

22   Foregoing the Ultimatums   107

23   The Unforgivable   110

24   Recognize Spiritual Battles   115

25   Reassess Choosing Death over Life   121

26   Know Someone is Fighting for You   124

27   Know We Are All Here   126

28   Know This Is Not the End   128

     References   130

INTRODUCTION

It seems we don't go many mornings without hearing of a Christian leader, role model or friend taking his or her own life. One particular morning in 2019 after I began writing this book, I learned of the suicide of Jarrid Wilson, an associate pastor at Harvest Christian Fellowship in California. In addition to Jarrid's pastoral role, he and his wife had founded an organization called Anthem of Hope to equip the church with the resources needed to better assist those struggling with depression, anxiety, self-harm, addiction and suicide. This was a personal project for Jarrid, who was open about his own such struggles. On September 9, 2019, he tweeted: "Loving Jesus doesn't always cure suicidal thoughts. Loving Jesus doesn't always cure depression. Loving Jesus doesn't always cure PTSD. Loving Jesus doesn't always cure anxiety. But that doesn't mean Jesus doesn't offer us companionship and comfort. He ALWAYS does that."[1]

That same day, Jarrid officiated a funeral for a "Jesus-loving woman who took her own life."[2] Commenting on Jarrid's post to ask for prayers for the woman's family was Kay Warren, wife of megachurch pastor and best-selling author Rick Warren and mom to Matthew Warren, who had himself taken his own life years earlier.[3] Sometime later that evening, Jarrid succumbed to his own struggle with mental illness.

1

These are tragic, yet not isolated outliers, and I fear that, as a reader of this book, you already know this. Suicide is taking the world by storm, and not only the world but also those who are "not of this world."[4] The increase in suicide within Christian communities is also slowly changing the way the church speaks about suicide, as well it should. Do not misunderstand—God and God's word in the Bible do not change; He is the same yesterday, today and forever.[5] In the past, however, death by mental illness has borne its own stigma and scars within the church, preventing families and communities from grieving wonderful humans gone before their time. Instead of comforting and surrounding a family left bereft by suicide as a Christian community body is commanded to do, the church has been the first to banish them, the first to question whether the person was truly saved or whether he or she could truly be in heaven with the Lord. That antiquated and irreverent approach must change if the church is to respond adequately and biblically to the increasing rates of suicide within the church.

In a memoriam to Jarrid Wilson on the Harvest Christian Fellowship website, Pastor Greg Laurie stated unequivocally that Jarrid Wilson was with the Lord after his suicide. "At times like this, we must remember that as Christians, we do not live on explanations but on promises. We fall back on what we do know, not on what we don't know. We do know that Jarrid put his faith in Jesus Christ and we also know that he is in heaven now."[6]

Before his passing, Jarrid had made his own defense. In a blog post entitled "Why Suicide Doesn't Always Lead to Hell," Jarrid addressed the suicides of public personalities Anthony Bourdain and Kate Spade. He wrote he felt led to post because of how many people were speaking out about the eternal destinies of the two. "The reality is, you wouldn't dare say that someone who died of cancer is going to hell just because of their illness would you? I hope not. Then please don't assume someone who died of suicide via severe depression is going to hell either. Both are illnesses. Both can lead to death. The deciding factor for someone entering heaven vs. hell in regards to Christianity is this: Knowing Jesus as your personal Lord and savior."[7]

If this notion offends you, please check your Bible. Also, if this notion doesn't offend you, please check your Bible. The Bible is our only hope for true discernment without the influence of culture and opinion, and when the words of this book and His word differ, always follow His word. I am confident that in your reading of either book, you will find no clause that excludes those who have died by suicide from an eternal relationship with a merciful God—just, as Jarrid might say, no clause in the Bible excludes people who died by cancer or any other physical illness.

As a sibling of one who died by suicide, I did not know where to turn in the days after my brother's unexpected death. I knew the Bible was the only true and constant source of wisdom, but I did not know where to start. The word suicide is not actually in the Bible, for example, so it wasn't as easy as finding a page from the index and reading a quick excerpt. Having grown up in a Christian home always surrounded by cultural Christianity, I knew parts of the Bible, of course. If I had to be honest, though, I mostly knew the good parts—the verses about a kind and loving God who had given His only Son to save us from our sins. But what about my brother's sins? Did God forgive those? And more importantly, did God ultimately save my brother from himself?

At the time, I was a member of a strong, Bible-based church that just did not know what to do. I had a small group of fellow believers who didn't reach out. Jarrid Wilson recognized this gap in the church's response to a hurting community. In the days leading up to his death by suicide, his organization, Anthem of Hope, shared Christian mental health statistics from LifeWay Research. According to those statistics, nearly a third of churchgoers say a close acquaintance or family member has died by suicide, yet 49 percent of pastors say they rarely or never speak to their congregation about mental illness.[8] Only 53 percent of churchgoers with mental illness say the church has been supportive.[9] If the church is supposed to be a body, why does it seem as though we are leaving many of our members outside the church doors to find solace in the world, a solace that will not last and that will never truly comfort?[10]

Even more concerning, what about the times when the church, as a place of at least general refuge and community, is entirely unavailable? During the height of the COVID-19 pandemic in the United States, for example, nearly 11 percent of adults in the United States reported seriously considering suicide in the past thirty days.[11] A whopping 25.5 percent of respondents aged eighteen to twenty-four reported seriously considering suicide.[12] While the church, inadequate though it may be in responding to mental health issues, was forced to close in the United States, a quarter of the nation's youth was seriously contemplating taking their own lives.

Fortunately, we have a fail-safe for when the church is unavailable, either by willful ignorance or government regulation, in the Bible. Admittedly, the Bible can be a bit intimidating and perhaps hard to approach when looking for a specific subject. I wrote this book to have in one place an easily accessible biblical portrait of suicide—that is, who do we see complete acts of suicide in the Bible? Why? What was the context? What was God's response? What are God's promises in light of or in spite of suicide? The Bible provides a wealth of encouragement and hope, and I don't endeavor to collect all of its resources here. What I want you to see is that you are not alone, that your loved one was not alone, and that if your loved one trusted Jesus as his or her Savior, he or she will never be alone again. Do not ever believe the lie—a lie that seems to circulate most prevalently within Christian circles—that you are on your own through the journey of surviving the suicide of a loved one. Suicide does not catch God by surprise, and its practice is sadly as old as the Book of Life.

I also wrote this book to give you the space you need to process your own grief and the circumstances of your own loved one's suicide with the words of the Lord and the substance of history. What you will not find in this book are more devastating examples of other suicides occurring outside of the Bible or assertions as to how you should feel now. Not only was your loved one unique, but so are you. It took me six years after my brother died to start to put pen to paper on this, but it was something I knew was needed within the week after he died. A natural researcher, I searched in vain to find a book that didn't overwhelm me with information on how miserable my brother must have been or share story after heart-wrenching story of other deaths by suicide. Such resources were just too painful. I felt helplessly caught between the silence of the church and the hyper-emotion of the world. I pray these next simple words bring you a feeling of safety and comfort in a time when you need it most, while also helping you see that although the Western church may be afraid to address suicide, God is not.

PART ONE: THOSE WHO HAVE GONE BEFORE

As you may know, the Bible begins in a setting many thousands of years ago with an explanation of the creation of the world we live in today and its first human beings. It may seem that was so long ago we could not possibly have anything in common with the first people to walk on the face of the earth. Unfortunately, we do: from the beginning, man has had the ability to choose for himself (or herself) in all things, and we have proven time and again we are not usually the best decision makers. We decide whether to choose God and His way or our own way. We decide whether to continue to live in this body. And in some cases, we even make that decision for other people, whether by their request or not. If the first man and woman on the earth were Adam and Eve, made innocent in the image of God, their firstborn son, Cain, was the first recorded murderer in all humanity. Mankind went from the perfect life in the Garden of Eden, where men and women were walking with God and at peace with all creation, to murder and running from God all within one generation. Only four human beings existed at that time, and yet Cain became so jealous of his brother, Abel, that he killed him. The Bible is only four chapters in and we already have murder within the only family on earth. These are not the Bible verses you see hanging behind your grandmother's kitchen table, are they?

In addition to the first murder, however, we also see a divine pardon. At that time, without the written word of God or the permanent intercessor in place, the Lord spoke directly to His creation. God knew Cain had murdered his brother. God was not pleased with Cain, make no mistake about it, but what is interesting is that Cain declared a worse punishment for himself than did God. In his guilt, Cain argued his punishment would be too great for him to bear, that he should be a vagrant and wanderer for the rest of his life, and that whoever found him was certain to kill him. But that was not what God wanted for Cain. There was a punishment for Cain in that God removed his ability to farm the land, but God also enforced a great protection over Cain. In fact, God marked Cain in some unknown way that divinely protected Cain from harm from anyone else on the earth (as by this time the population had grown). Cain went on to have a wife and a large family and presumably a long life. God is merciful, not only because that is who He is, but also because He knew and still knows better than any of us how strong the pull of sin is. As He told Cain, "Sin is crouching at the door. Its desire is contrary to you, but you must rule over it."[13]

What I hope to reinforce throughout this entire book is introduced in the very first few pages of scripture; specifically, that man shedding blood with his own hands—be it his own blood or the blood of others—is neither a surprise nor a novelty to God. God knows firsthand the temptations we face and the difficulty we encounter while in this world. The second, and arguably more important reinforcement is that God is more forgiving than man. We will see this point emphasized time and again throughout the Bible.

For example, consider the great King David, a man who committed murder, and whom we will discuss later in more detail. When David sinned by numbering his army to boost his own ego and sense of security, God gave David the ability to choose his own punishment. David had three options: famine, pestilence, or pursuit by his mortal enemies. David's response? "I am in great distress. Let us fall into the hand of the Lord, for His mercy is great; but let me not fall into the hand of man."[14] David was a renowned warrior, but he chose to face his punishment from God instead of man because he knew God's just punishment would be interwoven with a mercy and compassion man rarely shows.

When we sin, when we fall short, even when we take the lives of ourselves or others, we sin against God alone, not against man. We may disappoint man or make others sad or angry, but we ultimately answer to God alone.[15] And yet, unfortunately for our time on this earth, man is harder on us and less forgiving than our maker. Man can make us turn on ourselves, man can make us doubt our redemption, and man can make us question the choices of our loved ones we thought we knew so well. Fortunately for our loved ones who have gone before us, God is more merciful than we can imagine. Though we condemn ourselves, God is greater than our weak hearts, and He knows everything.[16]

As stories progress through the Bible, the characters and events become so relatable that if the stories used guns instead of swords and stones, and maybe a few other advancements in methods of torture and transportation, we could easily envision them taking place in the twenty-first century. Our ancestors from thousands of years ago seemed no better at coping with the disappointments, tragedies and overwhelming uncertainty of life in this world than we are today.

It should come as no surprise, then, that after starting off by memorializing the first incidents of murder, the Bible also began to memorialize incidents of suicide. As all scripture is breathed out by God and profitable for teaching, for reproof, for correction and for training in righteousness, there is value to us investigating the incidents of suicide the Bible shares for our benefit and instruction.[17] These stories, hard though they may be, should be studied and discussed, not swept under the rug in exchange for a more upbeat sermon. God put these examples in His message to us for a reason.

Each of the instances of suicide we review in this section is different in what motivated the individual to complete suicide and how he did so, and I will provide context and additional commentary for your consideration. But a common thread unites: desperation to the point of death.

ABIMELECH
JUDGES 9

The first example we see in the Bible—or even perhaps of all time—of suicide or suicidal intention comes from Abimelech in the book of Judges. Abimelech's suicide could be categorized as what we would now likely deem "assisted suicide," but of all God's attributes, splitting hairs doesn't seem to be one of them.

Bible passages, as with passages from any book in the world, are best given in context rather than plucked out and isolated. As such, let's first get a better idea of who Abimelech was. We first hear of Abimelech in Judges 8:31, which tells the story of his birth: "And [Gideon's] concubine who was in Shechem also bore him a son, and he called his name Abimelech." The very next verse following this announcement of Abimelech's birth relates the final scene of his father's life. His father, Gideon, had been a faithful military leader and judge of the Israelites at a time when judges were the sole governing authority over the young nation of Israel. Gideon was so revered among the Israelites, in fact, that the people had tried to make Gideon their king, an honor Gideon refused by pointing to the Lord as the true king over Israel. Upon Gideon's death, however:

> The people of Israel turned again and whored after the Baals and

made Baal-berith their god. And the people of Israel did not remember the Lord their God, who had delivered them from the hand of all their enemies on every side, and they did not show steadfast love to the family of Jerubbaal (that is, Gideon) in return for all the good that he had done to Israel.[18]

With the righteous leader deceased, and the people of Israel turning away from God, the stage was set for a power struggle in Israel and the ushering in of a ruthless leader.

Despite his status as Gideon's son, Abimelech was not an immediate shoo-in to take his father's place as a leader of Israel. Gideon had seventy sons at least, perhaps seventy-two if that figure does not include Abimelech and Jotham, the only son of Gideon younger than Abimelech. That makes for a lot of potential heirs to the throne. Instead of leaving leadership after his father's death to chance (or the will of the God of Israel), Abimelech decided to take matters into his own hands. Unlike his father, Abimelech's goal was not to point others to God but to make himself king. Abimelech first convinced his mother's relatives, who lived in Shechem, that it would be better to have him—their own flesh and blood—rule as opposed to any of Gideon's other sons, most of whom were unrelated to the leaders of Abimelech's concubine mother's clan.

Those relatives then convinced the leaders of Shechem that Abimelech was the best choice to lead. This was an astute political strategy on Abimelech's part because Shechem was a key city in determining the leadership of Israel. When Abram, father of all Israelites, was following God's word blindly going to a new land for a new people, it was in Shechem that God told him that was the land He would give Abram's descendants. It was there Abram built an altar to the God of Israel and the first seeds of Israel as a nation were sown. When Jacob, Abram's grandson, who changed his name to Israel and fathered the twelve tribes of Israel, returned to his native land after running from his own deceit, he stopped in Shechem, set up camp there, and erected another altar to God declaring there that God was the God of Israel. Shechem was not only centrally located within the territory of Israel but it also had historic significance to its people.

For those familiar with United States politics, it was as though Abimelech was trying to win Florida or Ohio—the so-called bellwether states that can swing the Electoral College and the entire election one way or another. And the leaders of Shechem bought in to Abimelech and indicated their support for him the same way political supporters do today—with money. Abimelech took the money, hired "worthless and reckless fellows," and then killed all his competition.[19] (Thankfully this is where his strategy deviates from current United States politics.)

In Abimelech's thirst to fill the vacuum of leadership, he didn't just persuade people to support him. He took out all of his brothers as potential opponents—or at least he thought he did. Abimelech killed seventy of Gideon's sons on one stone.[20] But one hid himself: Jotham, Gideon's youngest son. Then the leaders of Shechem made Abimelech king.

Jotham saw what happened to his brothers and knew he had to escape to save his life. Before fleeing, Jotham warned the people of Israel through parable that their deference to Abimelech was not going to turn out well. Jotham's parable painted Abimelech as the least desirable and the last chosen to be ruler, but one who could devour the Israelites nonetheless. Jotham even warned Israel its collaboration with Abimelech would be met with fire and destruction. God is not mocked; for whatever a man sows, this he will also reap, and sure enough, Abimelech's reaping began only three years later. After a few years in leadership, God permitted an evil spirit to develop between Abimelech and the men of Shechem—those who had previously supported him—as a means to avenge the bloodshed of Abimelech's brothers.

It may sound a bit strange that God would send or allow evil spirits. At first blush, such an idea seems at odds with the concept of a good and holy God. But God, as creator and ruler of the universe, can use all things to achieve His purposes. Even truly evil spirits, actions and efforts cannot completely escape the sovereignty of God. In this instance, Abimelech was a mass murderer of all his brethren, and God chose to use an evil spirit to bring about justice for their innocent blood. Abimelech's unjust gain was now coming due with the loss of Shechem's endorsement. It seems politicians fell out of favor in those days as rapidly as they do today!

As those with power turned against Abimelech, there was now room for a challenger, Gaal the son of Ebed, to emerge and threaten Abimelech's rule. At the opportune, divinely appointed time, Gaal started to question what right Abimelech had to demand people serve him. Not much else is known about Gaal, but he was likely a descendant of the Canaanites who wanted to cause a revolution. As Gaal stirred up animosity toward Abimelech, Gaal gained the support of Shechem's leaders. As you are probably aware, despite the familiarity of the vitriolic nature of politics and the fickleness of supporters, in those days, removing a man from office usually meant taking his life. When Abimelech heard Shechem was supporting Gaal, he grew sufficiently motivated to attack Shechem to ensure Gaal and his supporters stood no chance.

Abimelech was a take-no-prisoners kind of fighter, and his attack against his hometown was no different. He apparently held no sentimental memories of his birthplace, as he captured the city, killed all its people, then razed it to the ground and sowed it with salt so it would not be easily rebuilt. It was a strong message in response to the city's support of Gaal.

When Abimelech learned that all of the leaders of Shechem had not been there, but rather had gathered inside the inner chamber of a nearby temple, he burned that temple down as well and killed everyone inside. Abimelech had his revenge on the leaders of Shechem, but Abimelech wasn't done. He was on a roll. He went on to the next city and captured it. Undoubtedly hearing what had become of Shechem and wanting to preserve their own lives, the people of the city hid out in a tower while Abimelech marched upon them. When Abimelech went to the door of the tower to burn it down—with all the townspeople in it—a woman threw a stone on Abimelech's head and crushed his skull. In response, Abimelech "called quickly to the young man his armor-bearer and said to him, 'Draw your sword and kill me, lest they say of me, "A woman killed him."' And his young man thrust him through, and he died."[21]

In that time and culture, it was such a disgrace to be killed by a woman that Abimelech asked to be killed immediately after a woman had struck him. Perhaps Abimelech was in such poor physical condition—he had after all just had his skull crushed with a stone—he was unable to raise his own sword against himself, or even to fall on his sword (as we see later in suicides). Instead, Abimelech used the very man sworn to be his sword and shield, his armor-bearer, and ordered him to do the task. Abimelech directed his own death with his own sword.

Abimelech's suicide may be considered in the context of individuals who know their death is imminent and take the matter of life and death into their own hands. From the text, it seems clear Abimelech faced certain death and asked it to be expedited to spare him the humiliation of being killed by a woman. In reading this language, I could not help but call to mind passages in contrast. The Bible tells us repeatedly the Lord can be our shield when we are faced with a sword:

> But you, O Lord, are a shield about me, my glory, and the lifter of my head.[22]

> The Lord is my rock and my fortress and my deliverer, my God, my rock, in whom I take refuge, my shield and the horn of my

salvation, my stronghold.[23]

The Lord is my strength and my shield; in Him my heart trusts, and I am helped; my heart exults, and with my song I give thanks to Him.[24]

Our soul waits for the Lord; He is our help and our shield.[25]

For the Lord God is a sun and shield; the Lord bestows favor and honor.[26]

For our shield belongs to the Lord, our king to the Holy One of Israel.[27]

O Israel, trust in the Lord! He is their help and their shield.[28]

Many problems face us and our loved ones that we are unequipped to confront on our own without the shield who is intended for us. Should we be so surprised that when we don't have the shield we need, we may feel compelled to reach for the sword as Abimelech did?

Abimelech's suicide may be more predictable and palatable than most of the others we encounter in the Bible. After all, Abimelech lived a power-hungry life, spent his days killing his brothers and innocent townspeople, and was facing an imminent death when he demanded his own immediate demise. His death wasn't even unexpected: it fulfilled the prophecy Jotham had spoken after escaping Abimelech's first murderous rage. As unlikeable a character as Abimelech was, the Bible tells us that God does not take away life, but plans ways so that the banished one will not be cast out from Him.[29] God can redeem all characters, even power-hungry mass murderers, and even more God wants to redeem all characters. Whatever Abimelech was or wasn't, whatever your loved one was or wasn't, God is greater.

SAMSON
JUDGES 16

Samson was such an important person to God, and to God's purpose of rescuing His nation of Israel from the Philistines, that a pre-Christ appearance of the Lord Himself, as an angel, personally delivered word to Samson's mother of Samson's impending arrival. Until then, Samson's mother had been barren. Then one day, an angel of the Lord came to her and told her to watch her diet (literally to not drink wine) because she would be conceiving a son dedicated to God. This dedication to God would be evidenced by the son being a Nazirite.

Being a Nazirite meant Samson would not cut his hair, drink wine, or physically touch dead bodies as outward evidence of his dedication to God. The angel also foretold that this son would begin to deliver Israel from the Philistines. The Philistines were a new type of imposing force over Israel at that time, in that instead of beating Israel into submission, they were slowly assimilating its people. It was then and it is now inappropriate for the people God has set apart to live, act and love the same way the world does. God intended for His people to live differently; specifically, in obedience to His rules out of love for Him. With increased Philistine influence, the Israelites were neglecting this divine directive.

In any event, the woman's husband, Manoah, was so excited he begged the Lord to come again, which the Lord did, only to have Manoah panic they were sure to die after having seen God. This was not an unusual reaction, mind you. The glory of God is often witnessed in the Bible as so great that those in its midst know they must certainly die. That was not to be the outcome for Manoah and his wife, however. They did indeed give birth to a son named Samson as promised, and the Lord favored Samson as He had foretold.

It turned out to be a good thing that Samson had the Lord's favor, as Samson seemed to be a poor decision maker who found a fight around every corner. As a young adult, Samson chose a Philistine woman as his wife, which was not technically forbidden, but was in very poor taste given the Philistines were ruling over Israel and subjugating its people. It was frowned upon by Samson's parents, but instead of honoring his mother and father, Samson demanded he get his way. During the wedding feast, Samson's new wife manipulated him into giving away a riddle answer so Samson would owe his new wife's family thirty new outfits (wedding festivities are not what they used to be, thank goodness).

When Samson lost the riddle game, he went out and killed thirty men from whom he received the clothes he then handed over as due. In response, Samson's father-in-law gave his daughter, Samson's wife, away to someone else. Samson was so mad he burned down all of the Philistines' grain and vineyards. Knowing that Samson's wife and father-in-law were ultimately responsible for Samson's rage, the Philistines turned on them before going after Samson. After killing Samson's in-laws, the Philistines captured Samson. But he did not stay a captive for long. Shortly thereafter, Samson broke through the ropes tying his hands and killed no fewer than one thousand men. He used only the jawbone of a dead animal—which he was not supposed to touch—and proceeded to make a joke of his feat. It may sound as though Samson must have been seriously into CrossFit. In actuality, God was with him giving him strength and favor.

As many strengths as Samson had, he had just as many weaknesses. This strong, favored man foretold to his mother by the Lord Himself not only had a thing for the enemy's women but he also had a thing for prostitutes. This is not the Sunday school Samson you remember, is it? Wouldn't want your child drawing a strong man eating honey from a lion if international hookers were in the picture as well, would you? He won't be the last biblical character we see tamed and made more palatable to fit the image we'd like to create of our heroes. As for Samson, he fell in love with such a woman named Delilah and visited her daily.

Unfortunately, the Philistines knew of Samson's weakness, and they started using Delilah to determine where Samson received his strength. Samson knew she was doing this too; it was not a secret. The Philistines were always at Delilah's trying to capture him. Even so, Samson kept returning. Eventually Delilah wore Samson down, or, as many men may characterize it, she nagged him until he could not bear it any longer. Samson confessed his source of strength was his hair. It is unclear whether Samson truly knew or believed losing his hair would cost him his strength. After all, Samson seemed surprised when his strength actually did leave him, and further, we've seen Samson surround himself with dead bodies, use the jawbone of a dead animal for some of his killings, and even eat out of a carcass, so it is safe to say Samson had already violated at least one portion of his Nazirite vow without losing his strength. If Samson could get away with touching dead bodies in opposition to his Nazirite vow and keep his strength, perhaps he thought the Philistines cutting his hair would not have any real impact either. His moral compass heretofore had not been particularly impressive; if anything, Samson seemed a man who did not really think through or consider the full implications of his actions. If things did not work out the way Samson wanted, he would take no prisoners in enacting revenge. This time, however, Samson miscalculated. When the Philistines called in by his mistress cut his hair, his strength finally left him. The enemies he had been destined to defeat even before his birth imprisoned him and gouged out his eyes.

I do not want to give the impression Samson's hair itself was anything magical or supernatural. Samson's hair was his source of strength because it was evidence of his devotion to God. When Samson's heart began to value Delilah more than he valued God, and wanted to please Delilah more than he wanted to please God, and trusted more in himself than in God's provision, Samson finally lost the strength of the Lord. Just as Samson's long hair had been an outward sign of his devotion to God, the loss of his hair reflected how his heart had lost sight of his true source of strength.

As He did in the beginning, God gives us free will. He is merciful and forgiving, but at some point He may not save us from ourselves and we will face consequences. Even when that happens, though, we remain less powerful than God and His plans. Our loved ones, even when they gave in to their final temptation, were not strong enough to override God's ultimate plans for our good and His glory. We see that in the ending of Samson's story as well.

The Philistines' treatment of Samson is what brought their downfall. As Samson sat in prison, his hair grew back. If I were the Philistines having just captured a man because we were able to cut his hair, I might have taken note of that. The Philistines, however, felt assured their god had delivered Samson into their hands and gathered to praise their false god and party. In another ironic twist, the celebration of their false god set them up for their death. All the leading Philistines were there, a crowd of three thousand men and women. In their festive spirit (which is a biblically diplomatic way to say intoxicated), they summoned their star prisoner, Samson, to entertain them. Blind though he was, Samson asked to feel the pillars on which the house rested. Then Samson called out to the Lord to remember him, to strengthen him, and to let him bring vengeance on the Philistines for blinding him. Samson cried out to God, "Let me die with the Philistines!" before summoning the strength to collapse the pillars and bring the house down on himself and more than three thousand Philistines.[30] Samson had taken revenge several times in his life, but his ultimate revenge came with his last act.

The Bible emphasizes that Samson's hair began to grow back in prison, but the story culminates in more than that: Samson calls on the Lord in his final moments. Samson did not approach his own certain death in his own strength, neither did Samson undertake revenge in his own strength. Just as Samson's hair had returned to him, so had his reliance on the Lord. Samson brought down what were undoubtedly incredibly strong and secure pillars because he called on God. He was ultimately able to die because he called on God.

What I love about the picture of Samson's suicide is what the Bible continues to tell us about Samson. Within sentences of stating that Samson called out to God to let him die with the Philistines and then acted on that intent, the Bible reminds us that Samson had judged Israel for twenty years. Further, the author of the book of Hebrews refers to Samson as one of the faithful judges of Israel who overcame adversity through amazing faith thousands of years after Samson's death:

> For time will fail me if I tell of Gideon, Barak, Samson, Jephthah, of David and Samuel and the prophets, who by faith conquered kingdoms, performed acts of righteousness, obtained promises, shut the mouths of lions, quenched the power of fire, escaped the edge of the sword, from weakness were made strong, became mighty in war, put foreign armies to flight.[31]

Samson, who murdered thousands, intermarried with his oppressors, and slept with foreign prostitutes only to kill himself as a method of securing revenge against his captors, was not remembered for his last act but for his life of faith. God and the future authors of scripture remembered him for calling on God in his final moments. He was foretold by God and set apart by Him, even though God knew all of the trespasses Samson would make up to and including his final act.

Samson, just like many Sunday school Bible heroes, was not all that virtuous. He heaped up bodies: Samson's death count was no fewer than 4,030 people, plus himself. Yet God counted him as righteous and used Samson as an example for future generations. In his life and death Samson brings us many great reassurances. First, you do not have to be perfect to be remembered by God as one of His own chosen loved ones. Samson was far from perfect and has gone down in history as an Israelite judge, a powerful warrior and a faithful hero. There is no doubt in my mind, or in the minds of any Bible scholars as far as I can find, that Samson is with God. His salvation, like all of ours, was secured by God's actions and God's calling and not by Samson's own. God's calling of His people, then and now, is an effectual calling that we cannot thwart by our own actions.

Second, Samson shows us that a lot can change at the very end of life. Before the Philistines took Samson to prison, he was sleeping with a mistress and valuing her over God. By his last thoughts and words, however, Samson confirmed his heart's return to the one true God. We cannot know if Samson's heart changed over nights in his prison cell or if it changed in an instant as he went to collapse the pillars. Either way the result was the same: a dependence on God in his last moment.

Finally, if Adam was an example for us that all of humanity could fall by the sin of one man, Samson was one of the first examples that the reverse could be true: one man could have the strength to save many. As God's word is always true, even Samson's self-inflicted death fulfilled God's foretelling that Samson would be a necessary force to begin delivering the Israelites from the Philistines. Samson traded his life, one life, for the deliverance of many people, God's people of Israel. Another thousand years in the future, Jesus Christ would do the same thing on a much bigger and better scale, and without the sinful past.

KING SAUL
1 SAMUEL 31

Saul became well known as the first king of Israel, but that position, as positions of power sometimes do, led him to a tumultuous end. In the book of 1 Samuel, we see that the young nation of Israel had long deferred to a strong, righteous man named Samuel as its leader. God had chosen Samuel as a judge, a priest and the general day-to-day leader over Israel—but not its king. As we know from Abimelech's father Gideon, God was to be Israel's king.

As Samuel grew older, he made arrangements for his sons to judge Israel in his stead, but his own sons rejected their father's ways and perverted justice. The elders of Israel saw this and used what they viewed as a breakdown in the system to demand that Samuel appoint a king. After all, the other nations surrounding Israel had a king; why couldn't they? Israel had forgotten it had been set apart as God's chosen nation for God to rule over its people alone as their king. Israel's rejection of the Lord as king was a sinful rejection of God's authority.[32] Israel had seen firsthand the disaster of a man appointing himself king. Even so, they insisted upon it. Samuel tried to warn the elders that it was a bad idea, that they would one day need relief from a king in authority over them in addition to the Lord God. The elders persisted and eventually God acquiesced. Israel wanted to be like all the other nations: its people wanted a king to fight their battles; they wanted a king to give them orders; they wanted a king, essentially, that they could see with their own eyes.[33]

Right on cue, in walked a tall, handsome man from the tribe of Benjamin named Saul. Saul first appears to us as he is sent on a mission to find lost donkeys belonging to his father. When the search proved unsuccessful, Saul's servant suggested they pay a visit to Samuel, who he hoped could tell them where to find the donkeys. The servant did not know, however, that just the day before, the Lord had told Samuel He would be sending to Samuel a man from the land of Benjamin who should be anointed as king. When Samuel saw Saul coming, the Lord confirmed that this was the man who should govern as king in answer to the elders' demand.

The first glimpse we see of Saul's heart is beautiful and humble. After reassuring Saul the lost donkeys had been found, Samuel invites Saul to eat with him, and then gives the teaser: "And for whom is all that is desirable in Israel? Is it not for you and for all your father's house?"[34] (That is ancient Hebrew meaning all of Israel's hope and future is in Saul's hands.) Saul is confused by Samuel's praise. First, Saul was coming to get guidance on how to find lost donkeys, not take over the country. Second, Saul is not qualified to lead the country. Saul accurately responds: "Am I not a Benjaminite, from the least of the tribes of Israel? And is not my clan the humblest of all the clans of the tribe of Benjamin? Why then have you spoken to me in this way?"[35]

If you're familiar with God's ways, you are probably not surprised God would choose to exalt a humble, lowly man. God has a habit of making unexpected choices so His power can shine. The very next day, after one dinner and a night of rest, Samuel, alone with Saul, anoints Saul king over Israel. He generously gives Saul signs as to what would happen on his day's journey, all to reassure Saul the Lord had indeed anointed Saul to rule His people Israel. These were not normal guideposts; Saul knew how to get home. Rather, these were amazing signs such that the very Spirit of the Lord would come upon Saul, and that he would prophesy and be turned into another man. God gave Saul an entirely new heart: a new heart capable of leading God's people and glorifying God. I ask you to meditate upon the path of Saul's life thus far. Saul was tall and handsome, sure, but he was from a small tribe and clearly not in a position to anticipate power for himself. While on a routine search for his father's lost livestock, he is anointed the first king of God's very own nation; he is given the power of the Holy Spirit; and he is transformed with a new heart. And yet within the very same book of the Bible we will see him take his own life. Samuel—one of the greatest prophets recorded in the Bible—exclaimed of Saul: "Do you see him whom the Lord has chosen? There is none like him among all the people."[36] Truly, it seems to me that if so great a figure as Saul is susceptible to taking his own life, who are we to be surprised we would not all be at risk of doing the same?

God giving His people a human king, however, came with conditions. Samuel also had to warn the people of Israel:

> If you will fear the Lord and serve Him and obey His voice and not rebel against the commandment of the Lord, and if both you and the king who reigns over you will follow the Lord your God, it will be well. But if you will not obey the voice of the Lord, but rebel against the commandment of the Lord, then the hand of the Lord will be against you and your king.[37]

Even though it was evil for the people of Israel to demand a king, it pleased the Lord to keep them as His own people. Like a loving father, the Lord wanted to give His children the reassurance they craved in a human king so long as they continued to rely on Him. The people and the king now had to faithfully fear the Lord and serve Him with all of their hearts to live in peace, as is required of us to this day.

As are the Israelites, Saul is such a relatable person in the Bible because his ups and downs are at once incredible and yet revealing of our own short memories and lack of trust (and patience) in the Lord. The Bible tells us that after Saul had reigned over Israel for two years, he offered an unlawful sacrifice during a particularly pivotal and frightening battle against the Philistines. Let me explain a bit here: in the Old Testament time period—that is, before Jesus Christ came as a perfect sacrifice that would last for all eternity—the Israelites were under strict rules for offering sacrifices that made a way for a sinful people to worship and pray to a perfect and holy God. Samuel, as a priest, could offer the sacrifices. Samuel had assured Saul he would join him in seven days and would presumably take care of the necessary sacrifices when he arrived. But Samuel was late. And Saul was stressed. The Philistines were coming at Saul and his men with thirty thousand chariots, six thousand horsemen and troops "like the sand on the seashore in multitude."[38] The Israelites knew they were in trouble and started scattering, hiding themselves in caves or outright fleeing. Saul, impatient and worried, offered a burnt offering that violated the commandments of the Lord. God took Saul from anonymity, gave him a new heart and spirit, and gave him only one job: to obey the voice of the Lord. And Saul could not do it. Just as none of us can follow or trust in God without fully submitting to the power of the Spirit, and just as we still give way to our flesh and the realities of this world, so Saul gave way. Frankly, I know I would have been no different. If I had my army scattering, a strong enemy coming at me and a tardy prophet who had gotten me into the whole mess, I would have been offering sacrifices left and right. Let's be honest—it is much easier to take matters into our own hands than to wait on the Lord, or to trust in the Lord, or to endure suffering. After all, we cannot usually see the angel armies fighting on our behalf.[39] And anyway, isn't this all Samuel's fault for being late? As someone who appreciates promptness, I would have been the first to lay the blame at Samuel's slow feet. If it's the priest's job to offer sacrifices, he should arrive at the time he said and offer the sacrifices!

Saul's failure to wait on Samuel and ultimately his failure to obey the setup God had established would be Saul's downfall. The wise Samuel (once he arrived) told Saul the bad news right away: "You have not kept the command of the Lord your God, with which He commanded you. For then the Lord would have established your kingdom over Israel forever. But now your kingdom shall not continue."[40] Nothing like showing up late and with bad news.

You might think that after this, Saul would renew his commitment to follow the Lord. But in chapter fifteen of the same book, we see Saul working the margins yet again. The Lord instructed Saul, through Samuel, to "strike Amalek and devote to destruction all that they have" as retribution for Amalek's opposition to Israel when the Israelites came up out of Egypt.[41] The Amalekites were descendants of Esau who lived somewhere along the path of Israel's exodus from Egypt. When the Israelites started their great exodus, the Amalekites attacked them. With the help of God, Israel defeated the people of Amalek. Not only did Israel defeat them then, God promised to wipe out the Amalekites in the future as retribution for coming after His people. But Saul did something we all feel inclined to do from time to time—he changed the instructions he heard to fit what he wanted to do. Instead of not sparing any as God had instructed, Saul and his men took Agag, the king of the Amalekites, alive and "the best of the sheep and of the oxen and of the fattened calves and the lambs, and all that was good, and would not utterly destroy them. All that was despised and worthless they devoted to destruction."[42] If I may come to Saul's defense once more, Saul had what seems a good reason for sparing the best: he intended to sacrifice it to the Lord. When Samuel chastised him, Saul seemed confused, saying he had obeyed the voice of the Lord. He did devote the Amalekites to destruction. But he also kept the best of their things to sacrifice to the Lord. Saul thought he could take the commandment of the Lord and make it better. But our God is not like other gods—He does not accept bribes and He does not need our input on His commands. He accepts obedience. As Samuel told Saul: "Has the Lord as great delight in burnt offerings and sacrifices, as in obeying the voice of the Lord?"[43] (Spoiler alert: the answer is no.) Once again, Saul was told his kingship was rejected on account of his own rejection of the word of the Lord.

Saul's continual disobedience ultimately caused the Lord to regret making Saul king over His people. As a result, the Lord moved Samuel to anoint young David as the king to replace Saul, setting up a dynamic relationship between David and the wayward Saul. Saul's successor had been anointed, but Saul was still king over Israel. Saul was technically still on the throne, but now standing calmly next to him was the young man ordained to take his seat.

Having once received the Spirit of the Lord and His favor, it was unbearably difficult for Saul when the Lord's Spirit departed from him. After Saul lost the protection of the Lord's Spirit, he was left open and vulnerable to an evil spirit. Saul faced torment from the harmful spirit and struggled to find peace. He grew paranoid of David because the Lord was with David— and everyone could tell—but had departed from Saul. In 1 Samuel chapter fifteen, Samuel tells Saul "rebellion is as the sin of divination."[44] One thing Saul had done in accordance with the Lord's commands was to remove all those who practiced divination (i.e., psychics and mediums) from Israel. But Saul had not removed or repented of the rebellion in his own heart. Saul did away with external rebellion without correcting the internal cause.

Saul's mental health continued to decline after the Lord removed His Spirit from him. We see example after example in the scriptures of Saul raging within his own house because of his angst, of having music played for him (by David no less) to chase the harmful spirit away, of hurling a spear (at David of course) in his fury.[45] If you have lived with mental illness or with someone who has it, you know it can be even more frustrating than a physical ailment. All of that unease is trapped inside without anyone able to see how much it hurts or to "fix" it even with all of our medical advancements and medicinal aids. I often think it would be easier for mental struggles to exhibit more physical symptoms so we could have something tangible to show where the pain is and where help is needed. Mental illness can be as catastrophic as morphing cancer cells and harder to treat without knowing how it is going to make its next appearance or how strong the onslaught will be. In Saul's case, for example, the next wave of mental anguish was signaled with the flight of a deadly weapon.

Saul's mind and soul were waging war against themselves internally even as his rage and envy turned outward to David. Saul went so far as to use his own daughter to try and lead David to his death.[46] David had found the love of both the Lord and Saul's own children, and he was upstaging Saul at every possible turn—you've never heard the story of Saul and Goliath, have you? Exactly. The loss of the Lord's blessing, the never-ending successes of his replacement and the spiritual torment by an evil spirit were all wreaking havoc on Saul's mind.

The narrative concerning Saul and David continues with David fleeing from Saul and then ultimately being in a position to spare Saul's life. Ironically, this scenario—Saul trying to kill David and David having opportunity to kill Saul but sparing him, only to have Saul recognize David's attributes—happens twice.[47] It's not that Saul refuses to accept David's new position; Saul recognizes that David is more righteous than he is and that David will surely establish the kingdom of Israel. But that's when Saul seems of sound mind. Saul cannot get off the roller coaster of acceptance, rage and frustration. Saul can see the writing on the wall, but that awareness aggravated his mental distress instead of relieving it.

The first chapter in the book of Romans shows us God takes an interesting approach to unrighteousness and sin. You might think God would remove Saul's envy of David, or dampen his rage against his successor, or finally give Saul peace in surrendering to God's way. You might even imagine God tackling Saul to the ground and making Saul choose His way. But God often does the opposite: He gives us more of the sin we have chosen.[48] As Saul persisted in his rebellion, God allowed Saul to lean into it even more. God chose Saul and gave him everything he needed for success, but Saul wanted to do things his own way. Unfortunately, God obliged Saul's desire. We saw this pattern at the outset with Israel's insistence on a king. God wants us to obey His way, but when we reject that way over and over, He eventually lets us do what we want.

When Saul sees the army of the Philistines pressing against him and the nation of Israel again, he was again very afraid. Saul tried to call on the Lord, but the Lord did not answer Saul or provide guidance. Saul no longer had Samuel to call on either, as by this time Samuel had died. As evidence that Saul was still not repenting, Saul wanted to take matters into his own hands once again. Saul had his servants seek out a medium for him—no easy task, given Saul himself had previously cast out all mediums from the land of Israel pursuant to God's instruction.

Please understand this passage does not condone seeking out psychics or mediums in an attempt to contact a deceased loved one.[49] Although biblical scholars have argued witchcraft puts the seeker in contact with demons impersonating those being sought since the dead person cannot ordinarily be contacted, this text does provide indications that allow me to argue that in this instance God allowed Saul to actually contact Samuel through the medium.[50]

First, even the medium seemed surprised at Samuel's appearance, which usually did not happen. Further, Samuel's communication with Saul was neither encouraging nor helpful, and it was most certainly not what Saul wanted to hear; you would think a made-up apparition would be more diplomatic and agreeable. Finally, what Samuel says to Saul actually does come to pass as Samuel describes. Samuel, perturbed at being disturbed in his peaceful afterlife, reiterates to Saul that the Lord had torn the kingdom of Israel from Saul's hands and given it to David as a result of Saul's disobedience. As to the battle at hand, Samuel delivers the additional bad news that the Lord would give the army of Israel into the hand of the Philistines.

But then Samuel also tells Saul this: "Tomorrow you and your sons shall be with me."[51] Oh how I love this. After I lost a loved one to suicide, this particular line became such a deep, deep favorite of mine. The next day, after taking his own life, Saul would be in the same place as one of the Lord's greatest prophets.

Please do not misunderstand. The Bible is very clear: in order to be saved into an eternity with God, we must accept Jesus Christ as the perfect sacrifice for our sins so that a just and holy God may look upon us and see Christ's righteousness. But if we confess with our mouth that Jesus Christ is Lord and believe in our heart that God raised Christ from the dead, we will be saved.[52] Further, once we have been saved nothing can take away our salvation.[53]

During King Saul's time, Jesus Christ had not yet been sacrificed. So what happened for those who died before Christ? Before the death and resurrection of Christ, the Bible indicates that death resulted in a person's soul going to Sheol. From the New Testament account of Lazarus in the book of Luke, we see a great chasm between Hades (for the wicked) and the Sheol of Abraham's bosom.[54] Even though death in the Old Testament did not result in immediately being in the presence of the Lord as it does today, there was still a separation in the afterlife—a good side and a bad side.[55] Those going to the "good side" are blessed and destined to be invited to the feast of God's saints and ultimately reign with Him.[56] Those going to the "bad side" will not end up in heaven with our Lord. To which side was Saul going?

Ultimately we don't know—as the Lord told Samuel, man can look on outward appearances but the Lord sees the heart.[57] It is the Lord who saw Saul's heart and it is the Lord alone who knows the ultimate truth. Scholars have invested years to this research and remain divided. But Samuel does not tell Saul tomorrow he will be in Hades or even in Sheol; Samuel tells Saul that the next day he would be with him, an Old Testament faithful. With him, who everyone can agree was in the good side of Sheol, in Abraham's bosom. This interpretation is further supported with the knowledge that Saul's own son Jonathan, who would die with Saul, would be there with both Samuel and Saul. By all accounts, Jonathan was regarded as a righteous man and in a covenant relationship with God's chosen successor to Saul, David. Even now Jonathan is regarded as a type of Christ in the way he laid aside a kingship that was rightfully his as Saul's son for his friend and brother David, much as Jesus laid aside His kingship so we may share in His inheritance. This is how, through study, I understand the passage. As always, I encourage you to read the word of God for yourself, praying in the Holy Spirit that you may have understanding of the scripture. But would it really be so surprising for Saul to be with Samuel? We know from the New Testament that once we have been saved we are filled with the Holy Spirit and nothing can snatch us from God's hand. Similarly, we saw Saul be given the Lord's Spirit, a new heart and the ability to prophesy in the name of the Lord.[58] Saul did fall short, go astray and even lose the blessing of the Lord, but did that impact his eternal soul? If Saul was God's elect, then Saul stayed God's elect regardless of the frailties of his flesh.

We saw how Saul struggled through the years—being tormented by an evil spirit and overwhelmed by jealousy of David—but it was ultimately the Philistines who brought Saul's journey through mental illness and despair to a climax. 1 Samuel chapter thirty-one depicts the Philistines fighting Israel and winning, just as the deceased Samuel said they would. The Philistines first struck down Saul's sons, and Saul himself was badly wounded by the Philistines' archers. Saul, seemingly afraid the Philistines would mistreat or torture him in some way (as would be standard for the capture of an enemy's king), asked his armor-bearer to kill him with his sword just as Abimelech had done. This time, the armor-bearer would not do it. Undeterred, Saul took his own sword and fell upon it. And then, my friends, he and his sons were with Samuel.

Lest you think Saul was a king just trying to control his own death rather than let the enemy overtake him, know that not all the kings we see in the Bible responded to a deadly blow in the same way. King Josiah, for example, was shot by Egyptian archers and knew he was badly wounded. He neither fell on his sword nor asked his soldiers to end his life for him; rather, he asked his servant to take him away where he could die in peace.[59] King Ahab was also struck in battle and asked his servants to take him out of the fight. He would later die in his chariot.[60] Suicide was not a "king's" way out or a coward's way out; it was just Saul's way out. His life and death were unique to him. After living in torment for years, Saul used his injury to end his life.

Other biblical accounts of Saul's death should be addressed to avoid any confusion. The Bible is inerrant, but it does include the lies and folly of certain people. For example, in the second book of Samuel, an Amalekite tells David a slightly different version of Saul's death. Chapter one begins by stating David had just returned from striking down the Amalekites. And yet an Amalekite came to David (heir apparent for Israel) after escaping the camp of Israel. It seems odd to escape with your life only to run toward your enemy.

This seems to be a bold move—a move you might only make if you thought you had information that could help you find favor with Israel's true warrior king (as the song said: "Saul has killed his thousands and David his ten thousands").[61] The Amalekite reported to David that Saul and Jonathan were dead. When asked how he knew this information, the Amalekite answered David that he "happened to be on Mount Gilboa, and there was Saul leaning on his spear, and behold, the chariots and the horsemen were close upon him."[62] The Amalekite asserted Saul had asked the Amalekite to kill him, and even went so far as to assert he had obliged after discerning Saul would not survive his own self-inflicted wound. And then, after killing Saul, the Amalekite stated, he took Saul's crown and armlet and brought it to David, undoubtedly to find favor in David's eyes. John MacArthur speculates that in actuality the Amalekite was just the first to come upon Saul's body and he saw an opportunity to take the crown and report back to David as a way to curry David's favor.[63] Assuming this was the plan, it backfired. David instead killed the Amalekite for claiming he killed Saul, who David still respected as the Lord's anointed. David himself seems to later indicate he knew the Amalekite was lying about Saul's death, though the Bible does not explain exactly how David was so certain. We also know from scripture that Saul's armor-bearer saw Saul die—with no mention of any Amalekite—and did not follow his master in death until he knew Saul was dead.

Another confusing statement occurs in 2 Samuel 21:12, when the Bible states David took the bones of Saul from the public square of Beth-shan, where the Philistines had hanged them on the day the Philistines "struck down" Saul on Gilboa. As always, I encourage you to read the scriptures for yourself and earnestly seek the Lord's wisdom. No book can replace the Bible itself. But as my goal in this book is to expose the suicides in the Bible and the surrounding context, I do want to explain that in my understanding this does not mean the Philistines killed Saul by hanging. As we saw in Saul's suicide, Saul was badly injured—that is, "struck down" in battle by the Philistine's archers. Before the Philistines could capture him, Saul took matters into his own hands (after his armor-bearer declined his request, that is). It is possible that in finding the bodies of Saul and his sons, the Philistines would have hanged them in the town square as evidence of their prowess and defeat over an enemy king. It is also possible the Philistines may not have known they were not ultimately responsible for the death of Saul, given that Saul completed his suicide while in battle with the Philistines and that others could have tampered with Saul's body after his death. In context, David was receiving the bodies of Saul and his sons so he could provide them a proper burial in the land of Saul's ancestors. After Saul died, and perhaps after the Philistines even claimed responsibility for Saul's death or showcased the bodies of Saul and his three sons, valiant men had taken the bones of the deceased and buried them out of respect for Saul, but Saul and his sons were not laid to rest with their ancestors. They were not where Saul, the Lord's chosen and a king of Israel, should be buried.

Interestingly, the Lord Himself took ultimate responsibility for Saul's death, as we see in the book of 1 Chronicles, a recounting that also confirms Saul's suicide.[64] We learn in 1 Chronicles that even though Saul died by his own hands, the Lord claimed Saul's suicide was in actuality a result of Saul repeatedly failing to keep the Lord's word and seeking the counsel of a medium.[65] This is yet another reason Saul's suicide is such a complex portrait in scripture: not only do multiple parties claim culpability for Saul's death, but the God who gave Saul life also steps forward to assert His authority over Saul's suicide. Isn't that the case with every death, though? The Bible tells us our days are determined and the Lord has appointed our time limit on the earth that we cannot pass.[66] God wrote every single one of our days in a book before we lived even one.[67] In Saul's case in particular, we see the Lord removed His spirit from Saul because of Saul's continual disobedience. This removal of the Lord's Spirit of peace led Saul into despair and ultimately put him in a position where Saul felt he had no other way out. But God knew that in advance. God knew the number of Saul's days even before Saul was appointed king. And yet God still chose to love Saul and gave Saul His very Spirit. God knew the number of your loved one's days even before they decided they had no other way out. It would not have stopped God from loving them or giving them His Spirit.

KING SAUL'S ARMOR BEARER
1 SAMUEL 31

The scripture tells us rather abruptly that when Saul's armor-bearer saw Saul was dead, he fell upon his own sword and died with him. We saw earlier that Abimelech asked for death at the hand of his armor-bearer. Abimelech's armor-bearer obliged, but Saul's armor-bearer was unable to pull the sword on a man he was committed to protecting, saving it, rather, for himself. The Bible tells us Saul's armor-bearer could not kill Saul because he "feared greatly."[68] It is unclear exactly what the armor-bearer feared. Killing the Lord's anointed? Killing the man he was sworn to protect? Given that the armor-bearer refused to kill Saul out of fear and then had the fortitude to promptly turn his sword on himself, the armor-bearer's fear must have been closely intertwined with his respect for Saul and Saul's position over Israel. Such an emotional response also provides a glimpse into why the armor-bearer would commit suicide after seeing that of his master.

The role of armor-bearer in the Old Testament was a greatly esteemed one, held by important men. The armor-bearer who died with Saul was not Saul's first armor-bearer. Shortly after Samuel anointed David, Saul made David his armor-bearer because Saul loved David greatly. Prior to his interview, if you will, David's qualifications for armor-bearer were touted as him being "skillful in playing [the lyre], a man of valor, a man of war, prudent in speech, and a man of good presence, and the Lord is with him."[69] Oh, and David also happened to be the next king. That's not exactly an insignificant résumé to bring to a position. Apparently the role of armor-bearer was given such import applicants needed an impressive background. The armor-bearer was truly someone a king could trust with his own life, the man who carried the king's weaponry (literally bearing the king's armor) and who also, especially in the case of David for Saul, carried the king's spirit. The armor-bearer was the king's most loyal companion.

We see this also in the attitude of the armor-bearer for Jonathan, Saul's righteous son. In a story occurring well before Jonathan's death, Jonathan got the risky idea to go into the fortress of the enemy Philistines. His armor-bearer was the only one who went with him while the rest of the soldiers and Saul himself stayed behind. Jonathan's armor-bearer told Jonathan: "Do all that is in your heart. Do as you wish. Behold, I am with you heart and soul."[70] And as the Philistines fell before Jonathan, his armor-bearer was right behind him, killing the enemy on his master's behalf. This was no small role the armor-bearer was playing—God used Jonathan and his armor-bearer to save Israel from the Philistines that day.

We do not know the name of this man who became Saul's armor-bearer after David, but we can assume he was also a reputable and trustworthy man who God could have used, along with Saul, to save Israel. Unfortunately, his whole life was so lost in the life of Saul that when Saul died, the armor-bearer seemed to have no thought except to join him in death.

AHITHOPHEL
2 SAMUEL 17

We first meet Ahithophel the Gilonite in 2 Samuel 15:12. By this time, David is in place as Saul's better replacement and Ahithophel is serving as his counselor. We are not told much about Ahithophel's background or qualifications for becoming counselor to David, but we know he was the father to Eliam and thus seemingly the grandfather of Bathsheba with whom King David had his affair.[71] Perhaps Ahithophel's relation to Bathsheba, David's mistress-turned-wife, was how Ahithophel grew close enough to David to counsel him and hold such an esteemed position.

Ahithophel's closeness to David also made him a desirable target for a conspiracy against the rightful king, which was just what King David's son had in mind. Absalom, David's handsome and once estranged son, was planning a revolt against his father through which Absalom himself could be elevated to king in David's stead. This is where we meet Ahithophel, as Absalom is gathering unwitting followers to pronounce him king. Absalom had gathered two hundred innocent men to go with him to Hebron, an important city located southwest of Jerusalem, for the announcement of the coup. In addition, Absalom specifically sent for Ahithophel. The fact that Ahithophel was singled out among two hundred nameless men showcases the importance of the role Ahithophel held within the monarchy. Less clear is whether Ahithophel started out as similarly innocent as to Absalom's intent as the other two hundred men, who themselves are portrayed as mindless sheep led into a revolt.

Regardless of Ahithophel's initial motivations for joining Absalom, Ahithophel quickly throws his support and counsel from David to Absalom. Ahithophel is eventually described as a coconspirator with Absalom. When David learned of the conspiracy, he replied: "O Lord, please turn the counsel of Ahithophel into foolishness."[72] Putting some feet to his prayers, David then sent his servant Hushai the Archite to join Absalom's camp, both to thwart Ahithophel's counsel and to send word back to David of Absalom's actions.

It seems the Lord may have answered David's prayer as Ahithophel does not get off to a particularly positive start in counseling Absalom. Absalom was able to force David to flee Jerusalem, allowing Absalom to arrive in the overthrown city with Ahithophel in tow. Absalom then turns to Ahithophel for his wise counsel. They are in the middle of overthrowing the government, of running Absalom's own father and the chosen one of God out of town, and what does Ahithophel suggest? That Absalom go into his father's concubines in front of everyone. Of course there was a motive behind this cunning and unsavory advice. Ahithophel said such an action would make Absalom a "stench" to David and it would lead to Israel rallying around Absalom.[73] Because Ahithophel's counsel was so esteemed, both by David and by Absalom, Absalom followed Ahithophel's advice. The Bible tells us the counsel of Ahithophel was so highly regarded, in fact, it was as if one was consulting the word of God. Not that Ahithophel did consult the word of God, but Ahithophel was so important to the kings he was counseling they felt as if he was speaking for God Himself. That is an important distinction. It reminds me of another Old Testament recounting of a disobedient prophet in 1 Kings 13. It is outside of our scope here, but in short, a disobedient prophet lies to an honest prophet about what he heard from God. As a result, the good prophet does what the disobedient prophet said and dies. A good prophet, a good person, can be led astray by advice that is either intentionally or negligently misleading. In this situation, Absalom is far from good or honest, so it is not terribly surprising Ahithophel's disconcerting advice would lead him astray.

In our day and age, we are fortunate to have something else Absalom did not have: the full and complete actual word of God we can and should use to verify the advice given us by man to determine whether it is truly good and godly advice. Please always be thoughtful and consider whether you are taking the advice of God or of man, and if man, stop and consult the word of God. Go directly to God yourself in prayer. This is a privilege we now have through Jesus to help thwart the foolish advice of others.

Unfortunately, we'll soon see that Ahithophel's shortsighted advice did not just harm Absalom. Ahithophel's next idea was to pursue David and kill him that very night. Something made Absalom hesitate, though, before accepting Ahithophel's advice again, and he ultimately decided to ask Hushai for a second opinion. Hushai, as a mole for King David, of course discouraged Absalom against this plan. As guided by the Lord, Absalom decided to follow Hushai's advice instead. Because of that one small decision, the Bible says, "When Ahithophel saw that his counsel was not followed, he saddled his donkey and went off home to his own city. He set his house in order and hanged himself, and he died and was buried in the tomb of his father."[74] Ahithophel put too much stock on being the man who advised the kings and fell too hard when his advice was not accepted.

When I read this text, it reminds me of the first commandment: "You shall have no other gods before me."[75] Whenever we make other gods, or make ourselves our god, then we expose ourselves to extreme

41

disappointment when all man-made gods fall short. It is never if man-made gods fall short, it is always when. The biblical text links the events: when Ahithophel saw his advice was not followed, he went to his house and killed himself. There could of course have been other concerns on Ahithophel's mind. Perhaps he somehow knew—he was a counselor after all—that it was likely David would ultimately triumph over Absalom, and Ahithophel would be punished for his treason. That is not what the text says, however. Instead, the text directly associates Ahithophel's advice not being followed and his consequential suicide.

Does it strike you as odd that Ahithophel, a counselor so revered as to have been chosen by two kings, would take his own life because his advice was not followed this one time? Should it? How many times do you read a news story about an individual taking his own life because of one dip in the stock market? Or because of the rejection of one significant other? Or because of one important deal going sideways? These are real examples of treasured family members who gave up their futures, seemingly due to the loss of only one aspect of their lives. But how many times do we think the same thing internally? We come to identify ourselves in a certain role, as an advisor, as an employee, as a spouse, and then when our boss hires someone new, or when we lose our job, or when we do something wrong or the world does something wrong to make us feel rejected, it seems as though the world has ended. But it hasn't. I promise you, it hasn't. What it has done is show you that God is not your God; your role is your god. Your job is your god. What someone else thinks of you is your god. What the stock market does is your god. And these gods will always fail. It is very unstable ground. And when that ground gave way under Ahithophel, he felt he had nothing else on which to stand.

ZIMRI
1 KINGS 16

Zimri is infamous for having the shortest reign of any of Israel's kings, but even so we know that God places all kings and rulers in authority. 1 Kings 16:15 tells us Zimri reigned only seven days. As soon as Zimri forced his way onto the throne, others were justifiably working to take it from him.

Zimri was initially a servant of Elah, his predecessor as king over Israel (the northern kingdom), and commanded half of Elah's chariots. But one day when Elah had gotten drunk, Zimri came into his master's house, killed him, and seated himself on Elah's throne. Zimri then undertook to kill all of the rightful descendants to the throne, similar to Abimelech. Zimri seemed to go above and beyond, however; the biblical text indicates Zimri not only eliminated all of Elah's male relatives but eliminated Elah's male friends as well.

This action to slaughter any legitimate heirs was actually a fulfilment of the Lord's previous warning to the house of Baasha, Elah's father. God had warned Baasha that for all his sins and idolatry, his house would be destroyed. And through Zimri, indeed it was. Despite the divinely predicted elimination of rightful heirs by Zimri, his own self-appointment to the throne of Israel was not to go uncontested. When Israeli troops heard about Zimri's coup, the troops who truly represented Israel declared Omri, commander of the Israeli army, the next king of Israel. The army then besieged the city where Zimri was, and in response, Zimri, in seeing the city had been taken by Omri and Israel's army, "went into the citadel of the king's house and burned the king's house over him with fire and died."[76] This text describing Zimri's suicide continues, asserting Zimri's death was "because of his sins that he committed, doing evil in the sight of the Lord, walking in the way of Jeroboam, and for his sin which he committed, making Israel to sin."[77]

To understand Zimri's suicide, it helps to understand the way of Jeroboam in which Zimri walked. Jeroboam himself actually had a very auspicious beginning, being known as a "valiant warrior" according to some biblical translations and appointed by the great Solomon to rule over all the forced labor of the house of Joseph.[78] Solomon, however, as wise and favored as he was, had let his heart be turned against the Lord by all his foreign wives. For the sake of Solomon's father, David, the Lord did not take the entire kingdom of Israel away from Solomon's lineage, but the Lord did take ten tribes away and informed Jeroboam through a prophet those ten kingdoms would be given to him. Thus Jeroboam had the estimable position of being the first king over the ten northern tribes. Jeroboam was the first king of Israel after the nation divided—that is, after the nation split between ten northern tribes (Israel) and two southern tribes (Judah).

After becoming king, however, Jeroboam worried that if the people of Israel went down to worship in Jerusalem in the southern territory, the people would turn against him as their king. Even though a prophet had told Jeroboam God would divinely hand Israel's northern tribes into his hand, and even though the Lord brought that very prophecy to reality, Jeroboam doubted the Lord. Instead of trusting the Lord's plan, Jeroboam built two calves made of gold so the people in the north would stay in Jeroboam's kingdom and worship false gods, rather than risk them going to Jerusalem to worship the one true God in another territory. Jeroboam, an undeserving warrior, was given an unrivaled position as king over God's chosen people and did not trust God to keep him in power. The same prophet who had foretold of Jeroboam's greatness then had to tell Jeroboam of his sins, leading to his unenviable demise:

> Thus says the Lord, the God of Israel: "Because I exalted you from among the people and made you leader over my people Israel and tore the kingdom away from the house of David and gave it to you, and yet you have not been like my servant David, who kept my commandments and followed me with all his heart, doing only that which was right in my eyes, but you have done evil above all who were before you and have gone and made for yourself other gods and metal images, provoking me to anger, and have cast me behind your back, therefore behold, I will bring harm upon the house of Jeroboam and will cut off from Jeroboam every male, both bond and free in Israel, and will burn up the house of Jeroboam, as a man burns up dung until it is all gone. Anyone belonging to Jeroboam who dies in the city the dogs shall eat, and anyone who dies in the open country the birds of the heavens shall eat, for the Lord has spoken it."[79]

Based on the sins of Jeroboam, we can infer Zimri practiced idolatry as Jeroboam had, putting false gods above the one true God and casting the real God behind him. It is not dissimilar to Ahithophel's approach to God. When both Zimri and Ahithophel put something above God and that idol was then taken away, they must have felt as though they had nothing left. Of course with Zimri there were complicating factors. It is likely, for example, Omri would have had to kill Zimri to take over the throne. But the Bible does not say that the threat of Omri led Zimri to take his life; rather, it points to his idolatry as the reason for his suicide.

45

I spent some time living in Thailand, and it is easy to see the idols the Thais have made for themselves because they are actual, physical idols. It is not uncommon to see Buddha figures sitting in public (even outside of temples) to which food and drink are brought and to which prayers are offered. It is easy to look at these statues and point to a clear idol. What is harder, but just as important, is to find the idols we have created in our hearts. These idols are not visible to everyone, but they are no less of an idol than any reclining Buddha or golden calf. We may not feed our heart idols with tangible goods, but they are no less fed with our time and energy and devotion. Despite our audacity to think we have no other gods before us, I would argue we have a much bigger problem with idolatry in the Western world than do other cultures who bow down before physical idols. Is there something you could not live without? What would make your life nearly impossible? What if you lost your freedom, for example? Or your independence? Your health? Your significant other? What if there was a worldwide pandemic and you felt like you had completely lost control over your own life? We saw with Ahithophel and Zimri that their problem was losing a role or position that defined them. What if you lost your job or your wealth or your retirement fund? Could you continue? Would you have the mental ability to carry on in your own skin without that god?

This is not a struggle isolated to our loved ones who completed suicide or those who are contemplating it; this struggle attacks all of our hearts in ways usually invisible to those looking on from the outside. But there is an easy tell: you know you have an idol when you are worried or anxious or working with all of your might to control or maintain something. Our hearts have convinced us we need something more than the God who made the universe, counted the hairs on our heads and clothed the lilies. We need something more than the God who has taken care of the smallest detail (such as feeding the birds) and the biggest events (such as the end of the earth). We

46

need a relationship with someone other than the creator of the universe who offers to live within us. We need a provider greater than the One who kept an entire nation fed and clothed for forty years in the desert wilderness. It sounds absurd written out, but it does not feel absurd to the heart because the heart of flesh is so weak and so quick to deceive us. The problem with the idols upon which we fix our hearts is that they are not stable or constant or guaranteed, and when they fail us, our own hearts fail us. Our own will to live fails us because what we needed to live has been taken.

We are not privy to much of Zimri's background or history, but we are clearly told that Zimri idolized his kingly power and authority. He built himself a castle of idolatry and when that idol was taken away from him, he saw no choice but to bring the castle down in smoke around himself.

JUDAS
MATTHEW 27

The story of Judas's suicide is undoubtedly the most infamous story of suicide in the Bible. It is as heartbreaking as it is shocking for one of Jesus's inner circle to take his own life. It brings up provoking questions: Why would Jesus befriend him? And after befriending him, why would Jesus let him fall so far?

Jesus Christ called Judas Iscariot to be an integral part of Christ's early ministry as one of His twelve disciples in Matthew chapter ten. To say Jesus called Judas is to say Jesus gave Judas, who was identified at the outset and known by Jesus as the one who would betray him, "authority over unclean spirits, to cast them out, and to heal every disease and every affliction."[80] Jesus Christ instructed Judas to go throughout Israel to "heal the sick, raise the dead, cleanse the lepers, [and] cast out demons."[81] There is no indication Judas was not doing these very miraculous and supernatural tasks. In fact, it is safe to assume he was, otherwise the other disciples would not have been so shocked Judas ended up being the betrayer. Judas also had the peace of Christ, as noted in Jesus's instructions to His disciples upon their departure for their missional trips: "And if the house is worthy, let your peace come upon it, but if it is not worthy, let your peace return to you."[82] Jesus

48

sent Judas out as a servant under Jesus's own name with the authority to speak for Jesus. Judas was one of the disciples there to hear Jesus's lessons, see Jesus heal multitudes, partake in the miraculous abundance of food and most importantly, understand how to receive eternal life. Judas would have been there to see Jesus cleanse the temple, curse the fig tree and rebuke the Pharisees. Sounds as though Judas was in an enviable position, right? How could he do wrong when he was close to God in the flesh?

If you are familiar with the Easter story, you may know that Judas, seemingly out of the blue, sought out those who wanted to stop Jesus's ministry and asked them what they would give him to deliver Jesus. Judas, this man who just got back from going out to heal the sick, raise the dead, cleanse the lepers and cast out demons without even a bag for his journey or a change of clothes, was ready to betray the man who made all of that possible and see some profit for his treachery.

Why would Judas seek to sell his own master? We know from elsewhere in the New Testament that money and greed were an area of struggle for Judas. In John chapter twelve, Judas questioned a woman's anointment of Jesus her Savior with expensive perfume. Although Judas outwardly asked why the perfume was not sold for money to give to the poor, the writer shows us Judas's heart was not inclined to the poor; rather, Judas wanted the opportunity to steal the money for himself. Judas's line of reasoning concerning the perfume makes perfect worldly sense to me; that sale would have made some real money. It could have been sold for three hundred denarii, which would have been a year's wages for a guy like Judas. But even if the perfume issue could be argued in Judas's defense, why sell Jesus? The selling of Jesus was worth only thirty pieces of silver to the chief priests. That was, by contrast, not a lot of money. In Exodus 21:32, thirty pieces of silver was the amount of money paid to compensate an owner for a slave if the slave had been gored by an ox. In the prophecy of Zechariah chapter eleven, thirty pieces of silver was the amount paid to Zechariah for a month's work as a shepherd. It was some amount of money, sure, but not much. And yet Judas did not even negotiate the sum—so willing was he to betray Jesus that he agreed to destroy the ministry and the last few years of his own work for such a paltry sum. The money must not have been the true motive; rather, some motive outside of greed led Judas to betray Jesus. Those in charge accepted the cheap agreement and, with the plan hatched, Judas sought from that moment on an opportunity to betray Jesus. Shortly thereafter, Judas led those who wanted to arrest Jesus to him, and Jesus was taken away to be judged. The next morning, all the chief priests and elders sought to put Jesus to death and delivered Him over to Pilate the governor to institute capital punishment. As soon as Judas saw Jesus was condemned, he changed his mind and returned the thirty pieces of silver. Judas was remorseful, admitting to those in charge he had betrayed an innocent man. It was too late, though, and the chief priests did not care; they had the man they wanted. In response, Judas threw down the pieces of silver and went and hanged himself.

Interestingly, Judas's betrayal of Jesus was likely a form of self-preservation at the outset—a way for Judas to save his own skin. You see, when Jesus made His triumphal entry into Jerusalem on what we now know as Palm Sunday, Jesus was finally pressing the issue: the Jewish rulers would now have to decide whether to bow to Jesus or destroy Him. As part of Jesus's inner circle, Judas could have been locked up or killed for associating with Jesus. We see this creating anxiety in the group by the actions of the other disciples. For example, when Jesus told the disciples one of them would betray Him, they were all very sorrowful and "began to say to Him one after another, 'Is it I, Lord?'"[83] Each and every one of them knew they were in a dangerous situation and they were too weak to face what was ahead. They knew any of them might betray Jesus. And it was indeed more than one of them—Peter went on to deny Jesus three times that very night. So why would the very actions that Judas took to try to save his life ultimately lead him to lose it?

In some translations, Matthew chapter twenty-seven tells us Judas felt remorse for betraying Jesus, and that is a very important distinction when it comes to Judas's suicide. Judas felt remorse, not repentance; he felt the guilt of the world that leads only to death. We have all done things wrong, let people down and made sometimes irreparable mistakes. With no exception or exaggeration, we have all sinned and fallen short of the glory of God—even some of the most renowned biblical heroes, as I hope you are seeing in this book.[84] Not one of us has found perfection or been able to please everyone, please those closest to us, or even please ourselves!

Judas and Peter both betrayed Jesus in some way the night of Jesus's arrest, so why did Peter go on to become a key missionary and leader of the church while Judas fell to his own demise? The message of the Bible is the best in the world when it comes to explaining guilt, and few verses are more illuminating than 2 Corinthians 7:10—"For godly grief produces a repentance that leads to salvation without regret, whereas worldly grief produces death." Judas chose the latter path. He punished himself with a worldly grief that led to his own condemnation instead of a godly grief leading to repentance that comes with an added gift: freedom from regret and remorse.

The Bible states in John 17:12 that Judas was the "son of perdition," meaning he was the son of hell. We see at the Last Supper that Satan even "entered into" Judas, to be discussed in more depth later.[85] By failing to resist his temptations, Judas gave an opening to sin and allowed the devil to take over his actions. It seems Judas's fate was sealed as of that moment, though ultimately only God knows.

Would it have been better for Judas to never have been born, as

Jesus seems to indicate, because Judas was destined for eternal damnation? I believe God could have forgiven Judas—even Judas—if he repented and believed at the end. This should not downplay God's holy justice and righteousness but give due credit to the power of Jesus's sacrifice that it may always be known as so much greater than our sins. However, I cannot find the same reassuring verses about Judas as I can with King Saul, and I do not want to imply that I can. God wants no one to perish, but Judas was instrumental in providing our way to salvation in the betrayal and crucifixion of Jesus. Judas's betrayal was ultimately to fulfill scripture. If God is willing to use His own persecution and death to prove His word, then surely we can trust the promises He has made throughout scripture.

PART TWO: IN GOOD COMPANY

Before the coming of Christ, God gave His people, the Israelites, "the law" by which to live. The law served many purposes. It was, of course, for the safety and well-being of the Israelites so they could live fulfilling lives here on this earth. It also served to reinforce a notion we saw at the outset of the Bible: human beings on their own cannot live up to God's standards. Even when things were perfect in the Garden of Eden, man was determined to rebel. God made it as simple as He could; man needed to follow a handful of overarching rules to have a good life while living on this planet as exiles.

Included in those basic rules was the sixth commandment—thou shall not murder. This would include suicide, as ultimately the murder of oneself (as hard as that is to write). Interestingly, the Hebrew word for murder in the original text would have also included causing human death through carelessness or negligence, expanding the scope of those guilty of violating the sixth commandment. In the writing of the New Testament years later, we were given even worse news: any violation of any part of the law makes us guilty of violating every part of the law.[86] That was devastating to the pride of those self-righteous enough to think that because they had not technically committed murder they had kept enough of the law, that maybe they had been good enough, or at least certainly better than those who had committed such a grievous sin. Then came Jesus with the headline that God does not grade on a curve. Those who had failed to keep the sabbath holy were technically just as guilty of sin as those who had committed murder. Even before the New Testament was written, however, we saw how our shortcomings could all be interwoven: Cain murdered Abel because he was jealous of Abel and he was jealous of Abel because Cain himself failed to love the Lord God with all his heart. Cain broke two of the Ten Commandments (against covetousness and idolatry) as stepping stones to breaking the commandment against murder. We know from Jesus's teachings that Cain had broken the entirety of God's law in his heart before he ever took any physical action against his brother.

In the first portion of this book, we surveyed those in scripture who violated the sixth commandment with the taking of their own life. Unfortunately, far too many in the Bible violated the sixth commandment with the taking of another's life to attempt a comprehensive list. The Bible is quite possibly one of the most violent books you can read. Many biblical heroes were valiant warriors, continually faced with slaying Israel's enemy for the good of their people and the glory of their God. Those instances will not be considered in this next section. Instead, I want to share key stories of biblical heroes committing intentional murder against their fellow man, namely a few of those heroic figures who you would not think or refer to as men capable of such a heinous act. If every sin is a sin of the heart, then the condition of the heart that commits murder may help us understand the heart that kills itself and how God responds to any violation of His laws. The lives these men lived after committing murder shed additional insight into how God may respond to any violation of His law, up to including a violation of the sixth commandment, and how He may have responded to our loved ones.

MOSES
EXODUS 2

Even if you are unfamiliar with the Old Testament, you have probably heard of the great Moses who led an entire nation of people out of slavery. And if your knowledge of Moses is just through cultural contexts (such as the old movie The Ten Commandments that occasionally makes a cable appearance), you rightly see him as a biblical hero: a man who heard directly from God, led God's people out of oppression, and showcased God's miracles to an unbelieving generation. All of those are true components of Moses's life, but only because of God's grace.

Moses's story started out far differently. In Exodus chapter two, the Bible tells us Moses was a Levite, one of the tribes of the Israelite people. Unfortunately, Moses was born in Egypt during a time when the Egyptians held the Israelites as slaves. Despite Egypt's theoretical power over the Israelites, Egypt had become so afraid of the grand population of Israelites that Egypt's pharaoh commanded for every son born to the Israelites to be cast into the Nile. Without males, the Israelite population growth would naturally slow, and further, a lack of males would hinder Israeli military ability and prevent the Israelites from joining forces with an Egyptian enemy or rising up against the Egyptian military themselves.

As a result, when Moses was born, his mother hid him for three months. When she could hide him no longer, she put him in a basket and placed him in the river. She had no other choice. If she carefully laid him in a basket in the river where she knew certain people would be bathing, Moses had a chance at living; if she didn't, he would certainly be put to death. Providentially, pharaoh's daughter also had a divine appointment to bathe at the river and happened upon the basket. Pharaoh's daughter recognized he was a child of the Israelites, but took pity on baby Moses and rescued him. From the moment of Moses's birth, he was beautiful in God's sight.[87]

The Bible omits the details of Moses's upbringing and skips right ahead to "One day, when Moses had grown up…"[88] We know from later New Testament scripture that by this time Moses was forty years old.[89] On that day when the Bible resumes Moses's story—a mere nine verses from his birth in verse two—Moses saw an Egyptian beating an Israelite and Moses killed the Egyptian. Just like that! Moses was abandoned by his Israelite mother and seemingly rescued into a life of Egyptian privilege, authority and considerable wealth. Yet the first act the divinely written Bible wanted to showcase of adult Moses is murder. Interestingly, the Bible does not downplay Moses's act of homicide as a heat-of-the-moment, defense-of-others situation. Instead, the Bible describes Moses as having looked around, and only when he didn't see anyone watching did he strike down the offending Egyptian and hide his body in the sand.

We know from the first chapter of Exodus that a beating of an Israelite slave was likely a common occurrence: as a result of Egyptian fear of the growing Israelite population, the pharaoh had set taskmasters over the Israelite slaves to keep them from revolting. The Egyptians were to treat Israelites as slaves and to work them so hard the Israelites would have neither the time nor the energy to rise up against the pharaoh. From the text, it is also likely the Israelite slave beaten by the Egyptian taskmaster was safe at the time Moses murdered his abuser—the language specifically says Moses thought no one else was around, presumably including the then-released Israelite slave.

This intimation is further supported by Moses's surprise when two Israelites confronted him the next day. If Moses thought there were any witnesses, he would not have been as surprised word had gotten around. Rather, Moses was taken aback, both by the witnesses and by their response. Moses surely thought his Israelite brothers would understand his actions as avengement for them, but that was not the case. Instead, the Israelites questioned whether Moses was set to kill them as well. As a result of their awareness and ultimately of pharaoh's knowledge of the murder, Moses fled from his homeland.

Most of the time we do not focus on that part of Moses's life. We do not focus on the fact that Moses knowingly committed murder and then fled from the consequences. We instead focus on the Moses who was handpicked to lead God's chosen people out of slavery and into their promised land. Moses was not selected to lead God's people in this monumental task because he had committed murder, but he was chosen in spite of it. Selected examples of such scenarios are included in this book, but please know the Bible is replete with the trend of God seeking and saving and elevating the lost, not the perfect.[90] God uses broken people with shameful pasts throughout His word as a reminder that it is not our efforts, successes or merits that lead us to history-shaping accomplishments. It is God.

Moses ran away into relative obscurity, but God sought him out regardless and asked Moses to go back to Egypt; God had an important task for him. Would Moses have been able to listen to God and complete his task if he had stayed in his life of privilege as pharaoh's adopted grandson? Would Moses have been able to rescue the Israelites if he had stayed in his role as a palace insider? If God chose Moses to change history despite Moses's criminal past, why is it so hard to believe God would be forgiving to our loved ones who resort to self-murder in desperation?

Our loved ones may not have gone on to split the sea, bring water from a rock or successfully rescue an entire nation of people, but God never intended for Moses to be the star of those events either. God was the star of the escape plan for the Israelites. He just chose Moses, a murderer, to carry out His plan. God is always the lead actor, He is always the protagonist, He is always the climax. He will be for all of eternity. Meanwhile, He excels in the business of leading broken and sinful people into redemption.

KING DAVID
2 SAMUEL 11

When it comes to biblical characters worthy to emulate, few rank higher than King David, son of Jesse. We met David in our previous discussion of King Saul's suicide. We saw how David was plucked from obscurity, or rather, from tending his father's sheep in the field, and chosen to replace Saul as the king of Israel. In David's humility, and despite his divine appointment to the highest role, David rose through the ranks as armor-bearer to Saul and covenant brother to Saul's son Jonathan. When Saul cowered before the Philistines, small David stepped forward to protect Israel by killing an unbeatable giant with nothing but a slingshot and a stone.

Through David's obedience to God, he became a long-lasting king of Israel and the ultimate king, Jesus Christ, was born through his lineage. David was a valiant warrior, a skilled musician and a poet who drafted most of the praises and prayers found in the book of Psalms. David sought God, relied upon God and worshiped God. In Bible studies focused on David, I cannot help but feel insignificant and untalented in comparison. This man served as an unprecedented military leader, king of a powerful nation, ancestor to the Savior of the World, and had time to draft literature for the most published book of all time. Before you get too overwhelmed with everything David did right and all the ways God used him, you should know that even though King David is legendary as a man after God's own heart, he too carried out homicide, and not just in vindication for the name of Israel's king as we saw in the earlier discussion of King Saul's suicide. Rather, David committed premeditated murder against an innocent warrior in his own army in an effort to hide his sin.

Similar to Cain, David's sin also started with covetousness and soon led David down an interwoven path of lust, deceit and desperation. According to 2 Samuel chapter eleven, one spring when the armies would normally go out to battle due to the good weather and abundance of food supplies, King David uncharacteristically remained behind in Jerusalem and sent out his army with its commander. It is unclear why David remained behind that fighting season, as David often led the charge of his army. With the stage set for idle hands to become the devil's workshop, David saw a woman, Bathsheba, bathing on her rooftop and he lusted after her. Even after David asked about her and learned she was married to Uriah the Hittite, who was out fighting for his country under David's orders, David remained undeterred and took her for himself. When she became pregnant, David then tried to cover up his sin by bringing Uriah back from war and pushing Uriah to stay with his wife. David still hoped the baby could be passed off as Uriah's own. Uriah was just too upstanding a man, however, to eat and drink and be with his wife while his fellow soldiers were camping out in the open field and the Ark of the Covenant sat in a tent.

Uriah's mention of the Ark alone should have been enough to convict David; the Ark, after all, was the golden chest representing God's covenant with Israel. But you do not get to David's position without being resolute. David stayed committed to his deception. He tried everything he could—he got Uriah drunk and had him stay an extra day—and yet nothing could break Uriah's resolve. Uriah would not indulge himself. He was a warrior interrupted in battle and he was not going to go to his house to be with his wife. Uriah flat out refused to enjoy himself knowing he should be fighting for his country and his God. Compare that with the estimable David who did not even go out to battle in the first place.

David was king, though, and David could control the battlefield even from afar. After trying in vain to get Uriah together with Bathsheba, David determined his only other choice was to set Uriah up to be killed in battle. It seems an extreme choice, but we know that can be where the mind goes. Sometimes we can be in such a hurry to get out of a dreadful situation (even those we have created for ourselves) that we really and truly cannot think of any other option. It is likely these were the few days of David's life he did not spend praying and seeking God's counsel; rather, in a frenetic effort to cover one sin David could not stop himself from committing another.

David drafted a letter containing Uriah's death sentence and made Uriah himself carry the letter to the military commander on the field. David's letter ordered Uriah to be put out in front where the fighting would be the most severe, and then to draw back so Uriah would surely be killed. How cold had David's heart turned in the moment that he made a man serving him carry his own death sentence? To review: Israel's most revered and brave king begged off from battle and had an affair resulting in pregnancy, and then when he could not dupe his loyal soldier into shirking his battle responsibilities to help cover David's sin, David instead set him up to be killed. This is the man who wrote most of the Psalms, who is key in the lineage of Jesus, who demands admiration for his unwavering devotion and love for God. This is also the man who ordered another be killed so he could get away with adultery. As wicked as my heart is most days, I am glad that is the low bar being set. That is sadly a David I come closer to emulating than the giant-killing version.

Make no mistake—the omnipresent Lord was not pleased with David's actions. The Lord sent a prophet to David and made clear David had been in the wrong. David was not going to get away with murder. After the time of mourning for Uriah was over, David sent for Bathsheba and she bore David a son, but because of David's sin, because David "utterly scorned the Lord" in his heart and with his actions, the child ended up dying as well.[91] David had to face a temporal punishment. There was a consequence to his sin. But in no way did God give up on David or take away His love. There was grace and forgiveness from the Lord, for the Lord "put away" David's sin.[92] God did not change His mind and decide to have His son Jesus Christ born through another lineage. God did not take away David's status as one of God's chosen ones. God knew before the beginning of the world David would commit adultery and then murder to cover it up, and despite that foreknowledge, God promised David (and would keep the promise) that David's offspring would have a kingdom lasting forever in Jesus. God did not send David into the shadows for his sin, but kept David in the forefront of His eternal story. The gospel books of the New Testament deliberately traced Jesus's lineage to David and repeatedly referred to Jesus Himself as the "Son of David." God used the line of David, an adulterer and murderer, through which to send His Son, the Messiah, the Savior of the World. Once again God used an imperfect man and an imperfect situation to fulfill His perfect purpose of salvation.

In Psalm 51, we see King David's prayer of repentance to God for his sin:

Have mercy on me, O God, according to your steadfast love; according to your abundant mercy blot out my transgressions. Wash me thoroughly from my iniquity, and cleanse me from my sin! For I know my transgressions, and my sin is ever before me. Against you, you only, have I sinned and done what is evil in your sight, so that you may be justified in your works and blameless in your judgment. Behold, I was brought forth in iniquity, and in sin did my mother conceive me. Behold, you delight in truth in the inward being, and you teach me wisdom in the secret heart. Purge me with hyssop, and I shall be clean; wash me, and I shall be whiter than snow. Let me hear joy and gladness; let the bones that you have broken rejoice. Hide your face from my sins, and blot out all my iniquities. Create in me a clean heart, O God, and renew a right spirit within me. Cast me not away from your presence, and take not your Holy Spirit from me. Restore to me the joy of your salvation, and uphold me with a willing spirit. Then I will teach transgressors your ways, and sinners will return to you. Deliver me from bloodguiltiness, O God, O God of my salvation, and my tongue will sing aloud of your righteousness. O Lord, open my lips, and my mouth will declare your praise. For you will not delight in sacrifice, or I would give it; you will not be pleased with a burnt offering. The sacrifices of God are a broken spirit; a broken and contrite heart, O God, you will not despise. Do good to Zion in your good pleasure; build up the walls of Jerusalem; then will you delight in right sacrifices, in burnt offerings and whole burnt offerings; then bulls will be offered on your altar.

David's heart was contrite and remorseful. He knew he had sinned against God and sought God's mercy. And God answered. This is the same process God intends for us to follow today: to truly turn from our sin, knowing our sin may have earthly consequences, and to come to God for eternal forgiveness. No one in this world will ever be perfect; we have all sinned and fallen short of God's high standards.[93] But if your loved one trusted that Jesus alone was able to live the perfect sinless life, and then paid with His perfect blood to substitute Himself for us (as all sacrifice requires blood), then he or she was redeemed to a right relationship with God just as David was in response to his prayer.[94]

Your loved one's sin may bring temporal consequences, but for anyone metaphorically covered with the blood of Jesus, God remembers only the perfection of His son and not the person's shortcomings. In the end, King David committing murder does not tell us as much about King David as it does about God. Even though David's actions displeased God, God is once again shown to be a merciful and forgiving God. He, not David, overcame David's sin. He can overcome our loved ones' sin. He alone gives life. And He alone can forgive when life is taken away.

SAUL
ACTS 22

It is not uncommon for people to view the God of the Old Testament as an eye-for-an-eye God and the God of the New Testament as a God of love. First, you should know He is the same God. Second, you should know God used faithful leaders in both the Old and New Testaments who had the blood of others on their hands. The murders Moses and David committed were not excused because Jesus had not yet come; the violence continued after Jesus's ministry, death and resurrection. In fact, murders occurred because of Jesus's ministry, death and resurrection. For example, in the book of Acts in the New Testament, Stephen became the first Christian martyr. Stephen was killed for telling the people of Israel the story of their heritage and for showing them that the Messiah, Jesus Christ, was the promised one their own Jewish prophets foretold.

Christian evangelists to the Jewish people of Israel and abroad would share the truth of Christ with texts from the Old Testament to explain Jesus was the Messiah who fulfilled their sacred writings. The Jewish people who knew the texts well should presumably come to see Jesus as their promised Savior. Who knew these texts better than anyone? The man who was:

circumcised on the eighth day, of the people of Israel, of the tribe of

Benjamin, a Hebrew of Hebrews; in regard to the law, a Pharisee; as for zeal, persecuting the church; as for righteousness based on the law, faultless.[95]

Saul (later known as Paul), the man who had more reason to boast in the flesh than anyone, knew the Old Testament better than any of his peers. He more than anyone else should have recognized Jesus as the fulfilment of Old Testament prophecy. And yet, when Saul heard Stephen explaining who Jesus was, Saul's heart was so closed off to what he was hearing that he approved of Stephen's execution. Saul stood by while Stephen was stoned to death. Saul, the man who wrote the most powerful books on the mysteries of Christ, participated in the murder of one of the original Christian witnesses. In one of the many New Testament letters he authored, Saul admitted that when the blood of Stephen was being shed, he was "standing by approving, and watching out for the coats of those who were slaying him."[96] And Saul did not stop there—he continued "ravaging the church, and entering house after house, he dragged off men and women and committed them to prison."[97] After overseeing Stephen's death, Saul intended to take his persecution of Christians international. Saul started on his way to Damascus for the purpose of sending all Christians there to imprisonment and punishment in Jerusalem. That is when God entered the narrative of Saul's life and, as God often does, He rearranged Saul's plans. Perhaps because Saul's heart was so hard, or maybe because God's plans were so radical, God had to literally (though temporarily) blind Saul so Saul could finally see who God was. It is so hard for strong, successful people such as Saul to see God for who He is with physical sight that God had to first teach Saul to see with his heart.

The Lord did not leave Saul helpless, however. God reached out to Ananias, a Christian convert, to assist Saul, and explained He had plans for Saul. The Lord referred to Saul, who had just managed the stoning of the first Christian martyr and was in transit to make an example out of more

Christians, as a "chosen instrument" to share the name of Jesus.[98] While Ananias was afraid to assist someone who wanted to kill Christians, God knew Saul had already been redeemed.

My point in these passages is not to glorify or excuse murder, or to imply that God overlooks such sins. He does not in one sense; someone had to pay the price for sin, and that someone was Jesus. My point in sharing these passages is to remind us one single act does not define people. Even the significant act of murder does not define some of the biblical leaders we most revere. When I think of the Apostle Paul, I think of someone whose devotion to Christ seems entirely unmatched. Maybe it was, but it did not start out that way. Even the estimable and prolific New Testament apostle was not perfect and was not even always a believer in the Jesus he came to love. When Saul became Paul and changed from persecutor to proponent of the church, it was other people—other human beings—who were scared of Paul and remembered his sordid past, not God. God did not see Paul as a murderer, but rather as the fearless missionary he would become. God's mercies are new every morning; it is our fellow man who hangs on to yesterday's shortcomings. Ananias was fearful he was welcoming his killer into his home, but God was sending Ananias a new brother instead.

Throughout the Bible, God in His wisdom and mercy often steers clear of using the most prominent, seemingly perfect, well-educated and well-spoken people. If God had used perfect people to spread the gospel, the world would have attributed supernatural power to them in the flesh, as we are inclined to do now with celebrities and athletes and CEOs. Instead, God has used a lot of people of ill repute (murderers, prostitutes, thieves) to do His will and to bring Him glory so that no one would boast in the flesh but in the power of God. God sees the heart, not the flesh.[99] And for those who died with faith in Jesus, God sees His perfect Son, not their sin.[100]

PART THREE: A SENTIMENT SHARED BY MANY

Hopefully you trust by now that people recorded in the Bible—even those really important and intimidating figures—understood the despair and desperation you may be feeling now and that your loved ones may have been feeling when they left us. Some biblical heroes harmed themselves, some harmed others, but all actions were the ultimate tangible result of a condition in the heart. How often was such a condition present in other biblical greats who did not physically act upon the desire of their heart? The entire Bible, from Old Testament to New, speaks to the condition of the heart. It is the heart that receives the commands of the Lord.[101] It is the heart from which everything we do flows.[102] Jesus stunned crowds by equating murder with anger, but He knew anger from the heart would lead to murder.[103] It is the angst of the heart that gives way to the physical harm manifested, and many other biblical characters felt that despair even though they did not act on it. Many others in the Bible, and some we have already seen, begged for death though they would not ultimately receive death or give it. Despairing of life in itself is not a sin. Such despair may lead to sin, forgivable in Christ Jesus, but is itself not a sin.

As you will see in this section, even those biblical characters who had a close relationship with the Lord and an enviable witness of God's power still struggled with the misery of the fallen nature of this world, with torment from their enemies and with the many challenges that face those trying to live a righteous life (as well as the challenges that result from us inevitably and continually falling short of righteousness). In our arrogance, mankind has started the vicious and debilitating rumor that we should be able to make it on our own. The truth is you are not enough on your own, you are not doing okay by yourself and you will never be righteous enough to please a perfect and holy God. The beauty of such truth is that nothing more should be expected in this world. Popular culture may want you to believe that you are enough as you are, but the reality is that you are not. No one is. No one ever has been, save One. Even those who performed God's miracles on the earth during their lifetimes had to come face to face with the internal narrative that supernaturally confirms to all of us that we are "not enough" in and of ourselves to be good or pleasing or loved or accepted by everyone out there. That is not the goal. What a relief, because it is an unattainable goal! That is one reason celebrities and heroes and people who seem to have everything can still succumb to suicide as did our loved ones: because in our heart of hearts we desire something we can never attain on our own, and no matter what we do we will never be good enough by ourselves. That dejection is hard to sit with; it is hard to wake up to day after day. Even these biblical heroes whom God used to work absolute wonders—miracles—came to despair of their own merits and abilities. In many ways, we all have to get to that point of surrender and realization. It is from that lowest point that true life has the chance to spring forth.

MOSES
NUMBERS 11

How many times do you hear people flippantly say "oh, just kill me now" and you cringe inside after having lost a loved one through suicide? Well, it seems Moses may have coined the first serious use of the phrase. We already know some of Moses's background: briefly, Moses was saved from death as an Israelite child in Egypt, taken in by the pharaoh's own daughter and raised in privilege, only to murder an Egyptian and flee from his homeland. Moses's life carried on in the wilderness, however, where he married, had children and worked as a shepherd for his father-in-law.

While Moses was adjusting to a simpler, rural lifestyle, the Israelites continued to cry out to God to rescue them from slavery in Egypt. God heard the cries of His people and remembered He had promised them their own nation. In a selection process that makes sense only to God, God decided He wanted Moses, murderer and escapee, to return to Egypt and lead His people out of hundreds of years of bondage. Moses was understandably flabbergasted and incredibly reluctant. Moses had more than a few questions and concerns. God was patient with those concerns for a while, but when Moses continued to resist, the Lord became angry. Even so, God in His mercy alleviated Moses's fears and enlisted Moses's brother to reassure

Moses. The rest continues as did the Charlton Heston movie—the pharaoh refused to release the Israelites from slavery until God sent plague after plague to torture the Egyptians and eventually the Israelites were released from pharaoh's hand.

Such a climax should be the hardest part in Moses's leadership role, but the worst, it seemed, was yet to come. With the Israelites freed from slavery, Moses had on his hands a huge group to lead through the desert and to its promised homeland. When the Israelites left Egypt, the Bible tells us, their group included approximately six hundred thousand men. This figure would not have included women, children and all the livestock they could bring with them. Moses had been afraid to even speak to the pharaoh for the Israelites at the outset; how was he supposed to have to the fortitude to lead, feed and care for all those people?

The route to freedom and statehood for the Israelites was a circuitous one. In the end, the Israelites would spend decades in the desert. All the while, Moses was communicating with God, receiving His law, His guidance and His provision for the people. The Israelites were led by a cloud of God's glory, defeating adversaries and receiving food from the sky, but for them it did not seem like enough. They were, after all, homeless nomads wandering the desert.

The Israelites complained to Moses and lamented leaving Egypt. Moses in turn was becoming increasingly frustrated with the thankless Israelites. The Israelites wanted more meat, but God kept giving them more bread. Of course it was sweet manna bread that miraculously appeared every morning along with God's mercies, but after years in the desert, that didn't wow them. Finally, Moses could not take it anymore and he did what a lot of people do—he questioned God. For Moses, this worked a little differently, as Moses knew God responded to him in an immediate, audible manner.

Moses had heard from and talked with God. Moses had also seen God

71

perform many supernatural miracles. Importantly, he had seen the deaths of many unrepentant hearts at God's hand, and he would have known that asking God for death was not a request to take lightly. In Moses's experience, when he asked for something, God delivered. When Moses asked God to kill him, Moses was not facetiously saying, "Oh, just kill me now." Moses expected to die. Moses told God:

> I am not able to carry all this people alone; the burden is too heavy for me. If you will treat me like this, kill me at once, if I find favor in your sight, that I may not see my wretchedness.[104]

Such a sentiment is at the heart of many suicides: the burden is too heavy; I can't do this alone; I want to die. Sometimes that feeling becomes so overwhelming people feel they truly have no other choice. Moses felt that way too. After being rescued at birth, raised in riches, committing murder, fleeing his homeland to start a new life, being called by God Himself, witnessing unprecedented miracles, parting the sea to walk on dry land, and seeing food fall from heaven, he still said, "Kill me, God."

Can you believe this guy? How short are our memories and how strong is our flesh! Notice how Moses told God that if God had any favor toward him, if God wanted to extend any grace toward him, then God would kill him. Moses does not see death as something to fear or as a punishment from God, but as a gift and a showing of God's mercy and grace toward Moses. What is beautiful about this passage is not just the humanity and relatability in Moses's plea but also God's merciful response. Instead of striking Moses dead for his ungratefulness, God once again stepped in to respond to Moses's fears and shortcomings in real and tangible ways. Specifically, God did not just provide Moses with one additional helper, as He had in providing Moses's brother as a spokesman for negotiations with the pharaoh. This time, God anointed seventy elders to help Moses. God had Moses gather helpers and He shared the Spirit of God with those helpers so Moses would not have to bear the burden of leading the people alone. Remember, God had been speaking with Moses, supernaturally assisting him and guiding the Israelites along the journey. When God gave Moses the laws for the people, Moses spent so much time with God at the top of the mountain that he glowed. Moses's skin radiated the glory of God. Yet Moses still gave up. And once again, God understood the weakness of the flesh and mercifully provided even more assistance for Moses.

Fortunately, God is the same now as He was then. Unfortunately, we have the same shortcomings as the Israelites and Moses did then. When we are in the desert, how often are we able to remember the blessings we received on the mountaintops? Or if we can't even remember the good times, so deep and long is the desert trek, can we see the small mercies God is providing even there in the desert? For the Israelites, God provided manna every day. He specifically told them not to try and store it up or it would go bad. They stored it up anyway and it bred worms and stank by the next morning. The guidance has not changed for us. In Matthew, Jesus teaches us to ask the Lord each day for our daily bread—our daily manna. But usually that's not enough for us. We want to know what's going to happen tomorrow, and we get overwhelmed by those thoughts of what will, could or might happen tomorrow or the next week or the next year. But just as God set limitations for the Israelites, we are not expected to handle what will happen tomorrow with today's strength; we can only handle what will happen today with the provision and mercies God gives us today. His mercies that sustain His people now are similar to the manna that sustained His people then: new every morning and sufficient for that day alone.[105] If and when tomorrow comes, God has shown Himself willing to recognize our shortcomings and provide the assistance and provision needed to face that new day.

JOB
JOB 6

The story of Job is a popular biblical tale that has been appropriated, or more often misappropriated, by the wealthiest and most comfortable society to have walked the planet. I have sat in a downtown District of Columbia law firm while a wealthy firm partner adjusted her Hermes scarf, conference room lights dimmed to spare her recently touched-up eyes, and lamented over her Job-like existence.[106] The real story of Job involves the loss of much more than the creature comforts and superficial peace we have established for ourselves in America.

Job lived during Old Testament times and enjoyed a life of wealth and comfort while also being a "blameless and upright man, who feared God and turned away from evil."[107] But why wouldn't Job be blameless and upright? He seemed to have everything going for him—lots of land, lots of livestock (denoting wealth), and a big healthy family who actually enjoyed one another's company. This was not lost on the accuser either. We know the ultimate evil, Satan himself, is always looking to kill, steal and destroy lives and souls.[108] He continually stands before the Lord, accusing all of us in a futile attempt to dampen God's love and acceptance. That is the scene we are privy to in the beginning of the book of Job: Satan called God out on

74

Job, arguing Job could be good and God-fearing when he had everything going for him. Who wouldn't love God when He's given them everything they could possibly want?

Because God knows the heart, God saw more in Job than Satan could realize. God is omniscient; Satan is not. Even though Job was blameless before God, God allowed Satan to temporarily bring harm upon Job to prove Job's faithfulness. Satan, always anxious for the opportunity to devour another soul, jumped at the chance. Satan destroyed Job's property, wealth and children. And then Satan went back and attacked Job's health.

Job was a comfortable but blameless and upright man who feared God and who turned away from evil, who abruptly had his entire family, livelihood and health stripped away from him. Remember this devastation happened all at the same time—it was all going great until all of a sudden it wasn't. When it rained on Job, it poured. Job did not even do anything to deserve his sudden downfall. He wasn't dealing with the just consequences of his own sin; rather, he was caught up in the spiritual battle we know is always being fought.

As Job was sitting in ashes—both figuratively and literally sitting among the ashes of his former life—scraping his skin with potsherds, we get a glimpse from scripture of Job's resulting mental and physical anguish. The Bible deemed Job's suffering "very great," but what comes to my mind is "unimaginable." And how unfair, I think. It should come as no surprise that Job began to despair of his life. Who wouldn't? Everything Job had in his life was gone, and he was physically miserable in his own skin. His friends accused him of committing some great sin, some great trespass against God that would result in such utter devastation of his life as he knew it. Job, however, knew sin had not caused his despair, but such knowledge did not make the suffering any easier to bear. Job asked why he couldn't have died at birth. Job asked why he had to go on living. Does Job's distress sound familiar?

After this Job opened his mouth and cursed the day of his birth. And Job said:

> "Let the day perish on which I was born, and the night that said, 'A man is conceived.' Let that day be darkness! May God above not seek it, nor light shine upon it. Let gloom and deep darkness claim it. Let clouds dwell upon it; let the blackness of the day terrify it. That night—let thick darkness seize it! Let it not rejoice among the days of the year; let it not come into the number of the months. Behold, let that night be barren; let no joyful cry enter it. Let those curse it who curse the day, who are ready to rouse up Leviathan. Let the stars of its dawn be dark; let it hope for light, but have none, nor see the eyelids of the morning, because it did not shut the doors of my mother's womb, nor hide trouble from my eyes. Why did I not die at birth, come out from the womb and expire? Why did the knees receive me? Or why the breasts, that I should nurse? For then I would have lain down and been quiet; I would have slept; then I would have been at rest, with kings and counselors of the earth who rebuilt ruins for themselves, or with princes who had gold, who filled their houses with silver. Or why was I not as a hidden stillborn child, as infants who never see the light? There the wicked cease from troubling, and there the weary are at rest. There the prisoners are at ease together; they hear not the voice of the taskmaster. The small and the great are there, and the slave is free from his master. Why is light given to him who is in misery, and life to the bitter in soul, who long for death, but it comes not, and dig for it more than for hidden treasures, who rejoice exceedingly and are glad when they find the grave? Why is light given to a man whose way is hidden, whom God has hedged in? For my sighing comes instead of my bread, and my

groanings are poured out like water. For the thing that I fear comes upon me, and what I dread befalls me. I am not at ease, nor am I quiet; I have no rest, but trouble comes."[109]

Those are the words of a very desperate man; each time I read them I feel as though I am intruding upon a divinely poetic suicide note. Job was not done describing his distress. In chapter six, Job justifies his complaining. "The arrows of the Almighty are in me; my spirit drinks their poison; the terrors of God are arrayed against me."[110] Job continues: "Oh that I might have my request, and that God would fulfill my hope, that it would please God to crush me, that He would let loose His hand and cut me off!"[111] Job was in such despair that he craved death, either that he had never been born or that God would see fit to end his life. Job lamented his plight and his very existence repeatedly, even as Job's supposed friends continued to blame Job for his demise.

In Job's pleas, he did something unique and something man often struggles to do: he deferred to God. Job's desperate thoughts and requests to be put out of his misery were not complaints about God but were cries to God, as were his requests for death. Job desired death, but he desired it from God's hand instead of his own. Job argued with his companions in his own defense, but then he took his concerns and submitted them to the One who gave Job life and the One Job hoped would take his concerns away. The advice and counsel of Job's friends was fallible, so Job sought to speak to the Almighty; he desired to argue with God directly.

Job did not believe he would ever see a good life again. He knew he had received good things from God and must also accept bad things from God. The bad was so bad, however, that he cried out for death over life, which he now loathed. Job had the realization that our lives here on this earth are by their very nature "few of days and full of trouble."[112] As pessimistic as that may sound, such acceptance managed Job's expectations for his existence and allowed Job to be part of a bigger story. In Job's absolute pit of despair, where his relatives and friends had forgotten him, both his hired servants and wife were treating him as a stranger, and his own body was failing him, Job could still say that his Redeemer lives and that at the last He will stand upon the earth.

Come again, Job? God, who allowed your kids to be killed, your wealth and livelihood to be taken away, your friends and all your loved ones to abandon you, will be the Redeemer of this world? God has allowed your health to fail you so that you live in painful agony within your own skin, and finally you have nothing except a few supposed friends to berate you for all that you could have possibly done wrong, and the conclusion you reach is that God lives? I am incredulous that it is when Job decided his life was not worth living that he was best able to stand strong and assert that God can do all things and that no purpose of His can be thwarted.

All this information on Job's plight I am pulling from the very book God wrote and I cannot help but wonder why God would want this story in there. In my earthly opinion, it casts God in a bad light. In essence, God saw a blameless guy who was living righteously and told the enemy to have at him. As a direct result of God's suggestion, Job suffered, and Job suffered because of no wrongdoing of his own. Job suffered so much he wanted to die, and he could not imagine a world where he could see or experience anything good again. I do not know all the sufferings being experienced in the world right now, but I know some of them are unimaginably horrific. There are many people today, unfortunately including some of our loved ones, who cannot fathom they could ever again experience anything good enough to make life worth living. It is clear from the biblical text Job felt the same way.

I do not want to assert we should all expect to have Job's endurance to withstand suffering, but I am hopeful that we can at least turn to Job when we are asking, "Why, God?" Why me, why him, why would God let this happen? God never told Job the answer to that question, and you may feel as though He has not told you why either—a topic we will discuss more in later chapters. Yet here we are thousands of years later still talking about Job. I trust even if you are not a biblical scholar you knew of Job before you read this section. Through the story of Job we have a time-tested example of how God proved to Satan that some of His followers really love Him for who He is and not just for the blessings He has given.

We can be inspired by Job and reassured that while God allowed Satan to act, God only allowed Satan to do enough to prove Satan wrong about God's people. Satan was entirely wrong about Job's heart. Job did love God, and not just for the wealth God had given him. But it took suffering, refining and surrender for the best version of Job to arrive on the scene. And it took suffering, refining and surrender for God to multiply His blessings in Job's life.

In the end, God healed Job and gave him twice as much as he had before. And in the end, we are left knowing that sometimes good people suffer because even good people have a limited view of God's plans and purposes, of what the future holds and of what justice really means. Sometimes good people cannot see the spiritual battle or the divine viewpoint. Sometimes good people cannot let go of what they were enjoying to receive twice as much. Sometimes, unfortunately, good people, people who do not realize how truly loved they are, cannot withstand unbearable suffering to see the new character who emerges from the ashes of their former life.

It is also crucial to learn from Job that despair in itself is not sinful. When Job realized all he had lost, he was distressed, he tore his robe, he shaved his head—but he also fell on the ground and worshiped. In all his despair and emotion and crying out, the Bible confirms, Job did not sin. He did not curse God as his wife suggested he do, which would have been sinful, but he did cry out in absolute agony, which is not sinful. Human beings were created with emotions and feelings, and to have those emotions and feelings is not in and of itself sinful. Remember the heart is deceitful above all things, so it is important that we do not trust all emotions as truth.[113] Take those emotions and compare them with truth. Take those temporary feelings and compare them to the eternal word of God. But do not feel as though you need to suppress genuine emotion. Job was distressed and he acted out, but his grief and the emotions he felt at his loss were not sinful. Jesus Himself showed emotion while living on earth. Jesus wept upon hearing of the death of Lazarus, even though Jesus knew He was going to bring Lazarus back to life.[114] Jesus was in such anguish before going to the cross that He sweat drops of blood.[115] But He kept praying through the sweat. Even the perfect God in the form of man experienced emotions. Human beings can rightfully have emotions; we just cannot let emotions have us.

Thousands of years after Job lived, we were given a glimpse into how this world we now know will ultimately come to an end in the book of Revelation. You have probably heard enough references to the apocalypse and Armageddon to know a lot of really terrible events will come to pass—earthquakes, floods, water turning into blood, stars falling out of the sky, scorpions torturing men into inescapable agony. I always thought that surely if mankind started to see really bad things such as these happening we would all turn to God and submit to Him. The Bible tells us the exact opposite happens: the more unbearable life gets on the earth, the more man will blame God. That is a key distinction between the sinlessness of the emotions and response of Job and the sinfulness of man generally. When things became terrible in Job's life, he did not blame God. He had received good from God, and he was willing to humble himself to receive bad from God as well. Of course Job wanted out, as we've already seen. He certainly did not want to live in agony and despair. But the change in his life's circumstances did not turn his heart against God. As man becomes increasingly wicked until the end of time, man will become more tempted to curse God as Job's wife suggested and less inclined to submit his emotions to God.

Through Job's story of suffering, we know a battle is always being waged between good and evil to which we are not privy. Even if we do not always see or understand this battle, we may be involved in it just as Job was. We also learn that to have our emotions, such as grief and anguish, is not sinful. Our God has emotions, and we are created in His image. The great Job had emotions even to the point of wishing he had never existed and that was not sinful. If you are reading this book, I expect your loved ones had those same emotions. As we see from Job, despairing of life does not make God stop loving or caring for His creation.

Finally, we learn there will be suffering on this earth no matter how righteous we are, but in the end—the very end—faith in God will prove itself a worthwhile endeavor. While we are on the earth, it is not always going to seem fair. Sometimes the righteous will suffer, and sometimes the evil will enjoy worldly comfort and ease. To trust God even when there is no human explanation for doing so, and to trust that God enacts justice from an eternal perspective as opposed to an earthly one, is where hope can be found. Job did not take the ill-informed counsel of his so-called friends because he knew he could trust God when there seemed to be no reason for him to do so. It was an act of resistance to worldly wisdom. And although it may not be possible for all people at all times to withstand such suffering without sin (the flesh is very weak, after all), it is possible to rise from the ashes of a lost life just as Job did.

ELIJAH
1 KINGS 19

Elijah was such a dedicated prophet and man of God he did not even die; he went up to heaven in a whirlwind. Amazingly, the Bible also tells us Elijah was a man just like us.[116] While on the earth, Elijah served as a prophet of the Lord during a time when evil kings led the young nation of Israel into false worship of other gods. As part of his ministry, Elijah preached against the false prophets of Baal whom the king of Israel at the time, Ahab, and his wife, Jezebel, both worshiped.

The idol worship of Baal, as all idol worship does, was bringing trouble to God's chosen nation of Israel. In today's society, we would probably leave well enough alone, thinking that people can believe what they want to believe and not want to impose our own religious belief system on others. We may not even associate societal issues with our rejection of God, and even if we did, we would not want to be so uncomfortable as to try and share with others our belief in God. Fortunately, neither Elijah nor God minded being uncomfortable; they were both willing to sacrifice to prevent the Israelites from living a duplicitous life leading to moral decay and eternal death.

Elijah offered to put Baal and God to a competition to see which deity could bring down fire from heaven. In an unlikely showdown, Elijah went up against the false prophets as they called on Baal and Elijah called on the one true God. God showed up; Baal did not. After proving the fruitlessness of idol worship before all the people and showing the people of Israel that the Lord alone was their God, Elijah executed four hundred and fifty false prophets of Baal. The only problem with the mass execution was that the rulers, in particular Jezebel, had relied on those false prophets and did not take kindly to Elijah usurping her and her gods.

Jezebel had a problem with overinflating her authority, and she made a promise to Elijah to get revenge. Elijah knew Jezebel was not speaking metaphorically or having a temper tantrum. When she said she would kill Elijah, she intended to do so. Jezebel previously had an innocent man killed because her husband wanted his land; how much more was she willing to kill a man who had humiliated and slayed her gods? Instead of standing his ground and calling on the Lord again—the same Lord who had just brought down fire from heaven in answer to Elijah's prayers—Elijah fled in fear from the cold-hearted queen. Can you imagine? One day you ask God to bring down fire from heaven and He does it, and the next day you do not believe God can protect you from an upset queen. It never ceases to amaze how easy it is for our flesh to fear. Elijah must not have picked up on this irony: after being on the run from Jezebel for a single day, Elijah gave up and asked for God to take his life. One day! One day of fear and Elijah was out of steam.

Make no mistake. Elijah's request for death was not an idle thought from a tired or overdramatic prophet. Elijah's words had proven to have spectacular results. At the beginning of 1 Kings chapter seventeen, Elijah said there would be no rain for three years, and there was no rain for three years. Then, when Elijah prayed for rain, God sent the rain. Elijah's prayers did not stop during the drought either. During the same time period, Elijah prayed for the Lord to bring a widow's son back to life, and the "Lord listened to the voice of Elijah. And the life of the child came into him again, and he revived."[117] This is in addition to Elijah praying God would bring fire down from heaven, which God also did.

With that in mind, do you think Elijah glibly asked God to take his life? Elijah knew the greatness of what he was asking. He was afraid and ashamed of his fear, but he did not see another way out of his predicament. So when Elijah said, "It is enough; now, O Lord, take away my life, for I am no better than my fathers," he meant it.[118] He said those words expecting God to actually take his life from him, as God had answered Elijah's other prayers. That was one prayer of Elijah's, though, where God was not going to do as Elijah requested; God had a different, gentler plan in mind.

God did not answer Elijah's prayer to escape this world as Elijah expected He might, neither did God berate Elijah for making such a bold request. Rather, in that moment, God met Elijah where he was and nourished him with the simple things. A bit of food, some rest, and a whisper of encouragement was what Elijah needed to withstand that difficult season. Instead of granting Elijah his request to die, God sent an angel to Elijah with water and cake and the simple acknowledgment that indeed the journey was too great for Elijah alone. Elijah had just taken great and bold actions to defend God's glory, but went immediately into a season where he was in the proverbial valley of death. Elijah needed to rest and restore before facing the troubles of the world again. That is sometimes what human beings in the flesh need—not every day, not every season should you be expected to have the fortitude and the resolve to climb mountains. Maybe a bite of food, maybe some rest, is enough for today.

Elijah was discouraged and depressed to the point where he genuinely did not want to continue with life. Many Christians have arrived at the same low point. As Elijah was at his lowest, Elijah prayed to God expecting God to take his life, but instead God nourished him where he was. Not in the grand, dramatic ways God had responded to Elijah in the past, but rather in a still, small voice where God spoke to Elijah's heart to remind Elijah he was not alone. God brought a strong wind, an earthquake and a fire before Elijah as he was hiding, but He did not show up to Elijah through any of those majestic events. Rather, God showed up to Elijah in a gentle, lowly whisper. God was with Elijah, a man just like us, just as God is still more than willing to be with us and our loved ones and to give us everything we need for the season we are in now. God is committed to providing everything we need to stand under the depths of discouragement and depression.[119]

After spending at least forty days and nights in the valley with his fear and shame and a little cake, Elijah emerged with a new outlook, a new plan and a new helper. Generously, God gave Elijah explicit instructions and a successor to help him on the other side of his emotional valley. Of course it would be easier to make it through a season of depression if we knew it would only last forty days or there would be a good friend on the other side. A step-by-step guidebook and some of the cake the angel gave Elijah would be helpful too. We cannot always know these things; more often than not depression lasts a lot longer and is a lot more gradual in its release of our hearts. Elijah the great prophet had those thoughts too and was rescued from them by God—not rebuked by God, not scorned by God, not chastised or smote by God, but rescued by God. God is in pursuit of you, of your family members and of this world, even at its lowest point. He will be there in the valley if you listen for the still, small voice of hope.

JEREMIAH
JEREMIAH 20

Jeremiah was a great prophet in the southern territory of Judah after God's people split into the two kingdoms of Israel and Judah. Unfortunately for Jeremiah, he was a prophet at a time when God's people were turning away from worship of the Lord. In fact, the people of Judah had become so consumed with their idol worship and so unrepentant before the Lord, God had determined to allow the powerful kingdom of Babylon to take His people into exile. Given that context, it should come as no surprise that a true prophet preaching for God in such surroundings would not be a crowd favorite.

Jeremiah chapter nineteen tells us Jeremiah delivered a message from the Lord to the elders and senior priests in Judah, warning God was going to bring calamity upon Judah because they refused to listen to God's words. Such a message was not well received. It was so poorly received, in fact, that a chief priest in charge arrested Jeremiah, had him flogged and put in stocks, and then released him the next day. Jeremiah didn't stop, though—his resilience was such that he went right back out and repeated the Lord's message. I only pray we could be so bold in preaching the true word of God.

Jeremiah's resilient and tough exterior was not a full representation of all that he was feeling, however, as Jeremiah himself reveals in chapter twenty of his namesake book. The Bible tells us the Lord Himself put out His hand and touched Jeremiah's mouth to fill him with prophetic words. Nevertheless, after dedicating his life to warning God's chosen people to repent from their sins, Jeremiah had grown weary. He had been beaten and imprisoned. He had been utterly rejected by the people he had dedicated his life to saving. Jeremiah took his feelings, his dejection and his self-pity straight to the Lord who had ordained the prophet role for his life:

> O Lord, you have deceived me, and I was deceived; You are stronger than I, and You have prevailed. I have become a laughingstock all the day; everyone mocks me. For whenever I speak, I cry out, I shout, "Violence and destruction!" for the word of the Lord has become for me a reproach and derision all day long. If I say, "I will not mention Him, or speak any more in His name," there is in my heart as it were a burning fire shut up in my bones, and I am weary with holding it in, and I cannot. For I hear many whispering. Terror is on every side! "Denounce him! Let us denounce him!" say all my close friends, watching for my fall. "Perhaps he will be deceived; then we can overcome him and take our revenge on him." But the Lord is with me as a dread warrior; therefore my persecutors will stumble; they will not overcome me. They will be greatly shamed, for they will not succeed. Their eternal dishonor will never be forgotten. O Lord of hosts, who tests the righteous, who sees the heart and the mind, let me see Your vengeance upon them, for to You have I committed my cause. Sing to the Lord; praise the Lord! For He has delivered the life of the needy from the hand of evildoers. Cursed be the day on which I was born! The day when my mother bore me, let it not be blessed! Cursed be the man who brought the news to my father, "A son is born to you," making him very glad.

Let that man be like the cities that the Lord overthrew without pity; let him hear a cry in the morning and an alarm at noon, because He did not kill me in the womb; so my mother would have been my grave, and her womb forever great. Why did I come out from the womb to see toil and sorrow, and spend my days in shame?[120]

Jeremiah's lament reads very similar to the cries of Job. Jeremiah both praised the Lord and acknowledged His power, only to curse the day on which he, the Lord's prophet, was born. Jeremiah used the very lips God had touched to ask God why he was even brought from the womb if it was just to see sorrow and spend his days in shame. Jeremiah had an intimate relationship with God and had spent his entire life preaching the words God put in his mouth, and yet he still came to doubt the meaning and purpose of his troubled life. Jeremiah struggled with the rejection of his companions. He remarked that even his friends were waiting for him to fail, meaning he felt as though he had no real friends. He was surrounded by people watching and waiting for his destruction and doing what they could to bring it about. Jeremiah came to despair of his life. Is it any wonder? How many floggings could you endure before you start to question what God is doing? Even those steeped in God's wills and ways struggle against depression. The tasks and deeds God gives people to do, and the path we follow in life, is never guaranteed to be easy. Jeremiah saw that firsthand. Jeremiah had no friends and despite a supernatural mandate, he lamented his birth. He was doing God's will, but that did not make it an easy life. God's will for Jeremiah's life required a lot of perseverance and endurance from Jeremiah.

Many historians suspect Jeremiah also wrote the book of Lamentations, and as such he has been coined the "weeping prophet" because of his tears over the exile of God's people. Jeremiah had dutifully warned the people of Judah they would be carried into exile, but he was still discouraged to see it happen. Jeremiah also spent some amount of time weeping for himself. The writer of Lamentations lamented that God caused him to walk in darkness and not in light.[121] He lamented that God made him dwell in places so dark with emotion it was like being in the graves of those long dead.[122] God had walled Jeremiah in and made his chain heavy—torn him to pieces—so that he had become a laughingstock, his soul had no peace, and he had forgotten his happiness.[123] Jeremiah did not just lament, he anguished from within his pit of depression. Just when Lamentations could not get any more discouraging, the writer continued:

> Remember my afflictions and my wanderings, the wormwood and the gall! My soul continually remembers it and is bowed down within me. But this I call to mind, and therefore I have hope: The steadfast love of the Lord never ceases; His mercies never come to an end; they are new every morning; great is Your faithfulness. "The Lord is my portion," says my soul, therefore I will hope in Him.[124]

I have heard it said so many times: the Lord's mercies are new every morning. And praise God they are! But what is left out in so many contexts is what it took to get to that place of the new mercies and the new morning. Left out in so many decorative signs are the verses directly prior to that joyful verse in the story. The passage about God's mercies being new every morning was written during a lament where the human author just stated in the lines directly prior he has been filled with bitterness and rejected from peace. Joy comes with the morning, but often much weeping is heard throughout the darkest of nights.[125]

Do not let the world tell you your life should always be easy and fulfilling. Do not think sorrow and regret are abnormal. And do not let trite Bible verses taken out of context and hung on a wall shame you into thinking believers should always be happy-go-lucky. God is not a self-help pick-me-up; God is an eternal anchor. It is okay to feel down and it is okay to sometimes let it get the best of you. That happens in life and it happened in the Bible. It happened to prophets hand-selected by the God of the universe and given important tasks to be recorded and retold for all eternity.

But also see that it does turn around, just a few lines or a few chapters or a few books later. The weeping in your heart may tarry for a night, many nights or an interminable number of nights. Bitterness and rejection are part of the whole story, as is lamenting the corresponding heaviness of heart. It is indeed because the nights can be so dark that it is so miraculous mercies are new every morning. Joy will come in the morning, and one day there will be joy forevermore.

JONAH
JONAH 4

If you have ever read any of the Old Testament, you will notice a recurring trend: nearly every protagonist is incredibly forgetful. The people of Israel were, as a nation, forgetful of how God delivered and provided for them. The kings of Israel were continually forgetting it was God who fought their battles and defeated their enemies. The prophets of Israel forgot how God had shown up to make good on His word time and again. Jonah was no exception. Jonah, an Old Testament prophet, had just praised God with thanksgiving for rescuing him from certain death when he begged God to take his life from him because he thought it was better for him to die than to live.

Jonah is another biblical character of whom you have probably heard even if you are not familiar with the Bible because his story is so extraordinary. His story began when God told Jonah as a prophet to go and tell the people of Nineveh they were becoming too wicked and needed to repent and turn to God. Nineveh was a huge city at the time—the Bible tells us it would have taken three days to get from end to end with a population of more than one hundred twenty thousand young children alone—and would have been located in modern-day northern Iraq.

Preaching to Nineveh should have been right up Jonah's ally. Such a task fits the exact job description of a prophet and, even better, he was chosen to declare God in a big city with wicked people. If God selected me for a task that consequential, I would think I was very special. Jonah saw it a little differently, though, and did not want to go to the Ninevites. He ran away, God chased him down and had a fish eat him—same old story, right? I don't want to retell the Jonah and the whale story here, because as spectacular as it may be to live in a fish for several days before being spit out on the beach, Jonah's mindset during the entire course of events was even more unbelievable.

Amazingly, while Jonah was awaiting certain death—in a fish of course—he started praising God for hearing his prayer and saving him from his distress. Jonah knew he had run from God. Jonah knew he had done wrong. He also had no way to know he would actually survive his encounter with the whale's stomach. Yet he was already thanking the Lord for hearing his cries and rescuing him from the mess he had made of his own life in such a short time. And indeed, in confirmation of Jonah's faith, God did miraculously rescue Jonah from the belly of the fish. Nothing in this world listens to God's commands without question or complaint better than nature, so when God directed the fish to spit Jonah out of his belly, the fish did so.

To Jonah's credit, when God again directed Jonah to preach to Nineveh he actually did go the second time around. In fact, Jonah's short presence in Nineveh gives the impression he was the best preacher ever. Jonah had barely made it through one full sermon, one single cry out to Nineveh that the city was set to be overthrown by God, and the king of Nineveh demanded that everyone fast, repent and turn back to the Lord. In a very short time, Jonah has now had a near death experience through which he praised God for rescuing him before God even did so and had a huge sinful city seeking God after his first sermon. Jonah was on a roll and should have been feeling good about himself and his new lease on life. Yet Jonah's response to all of this was to ask God for death. Why was Jonah not praising God more than when he was in the belly of a fish? Why would he ask God to take his life from him so soon after begging God to rescue him? Why would he say it was better for him to die than to live immediately after an incredibly successful evangelistic trip to Nineveh?

The Bible does not explicitly defend Jonah's confusing response, but from studying God's word and seeing the emphasis on Jonah's reluctance to go to Nineveh in the first place, it seems Jonah may have taken something good and made it an idol. Jonah was an Israelite, a prophet and a patriot of a country of God's chosen people. The Ninevites were not. They were not from God's chosen nation. They were not Israelites. They were sinners, and apparently pretty wicked ones too. Jonah told God he did not want to go to Nineveh because he knew exactly what God was going to do. He knew God is gracious and merciful, slow to anger and abounding in steadfast love and relenting from disaster. God's grace for wicked sinners is the only reason I am still here. It is a really good thing for me. But how badly do I want that for other people? Is it enough for me to be saved? Or should I, if I really believe in God's love and mercy, want to share this good news with my enemies? That's where Jonah struggled too. Jonah loved being the apple of God's eye, but he did not want Nineveh to be saved. As rebellious as the Ninevites were in their external actions, Jonah was just as rebellious internally. Jonah's identity and his self-worth had become rooted in being an Israelite, a member of a nation chosen and set apart by God. Jonah was himself involved in the business of expanding Israel's borders to consume wicked nations, not convince wicked nations to turn to God and be saved.[126] Although pride in being an Israelite is a commendable quality as Israel was a nation serving the one true God, it is a slippery slope. The Bible reveals where that self-righteousness leads: it leads to the arrogance and self-salvation mentality of the Pharisees that Jesus was so quick to condemn. It breeds a mentality that you no longer need God's mercy or grace because you are good enough as you are.

Jonah's religious position and nationality had become an idol over and above the God who had given him those things. Jonah wanted what Jonah wanted, not what God wanted, and if that meant sacrificing the eternal souls of a large, rebellious nation, then so be it. Jonah clearly had not wholly surrendered his life to God, but rather Jonah had established a résumé and a plan he thought would be sufficient to justify himself. As a result, when God extended his favor to another nation, Jonah was so angry he wanted to die. Jonah lost his hope and will to live because his identity had gotten tied up in being superior to the surrounding godless nations and peoples. After Nineveh repented, Jonah was on equal footing with them. Where was his pride now? Where was his self-worth? What was his position in life if he had no claim to piety any greater than the common and wicked Ninevites? Jonah clearly had not realized or appreciated that our God shows no partiality and has no injustice in Him.[127] Instead, Jonah had hung his hat on being better than the pagans. God sent Jonah to Nineveh to tell the Ninevites of their impending doom if they did not repent. But along the way, God showed Jonah how his own heart hoped in idols. Jonah too needed to repent and depend on God.

The Bible does not tell us how Jonah's life story ends, but we do see how God responded to Jonah's request for death. Jonah was so full of self-pity he was angry enough to die. In response, the Lord did not strike Jonah down, but reasoned with him in ways Jonah could understand. God gave Jonah a plant for shade and comfort and then killed the plant, angering Jonah even more. God then explained to Jonah that if Jonah could pity a plant that lives and dies in a day, why could not God have sympathy for the great city of Nineveh? God took an argument Jonah would understand—Jonah's own—

and used it to illustrate His love and mercy. How amazing is it for a God who owed Jonah no explanation to patiently help Jonah understand and turn away from his anger?

Once again, the Bible presents a heroic character who is completely relatable, a character who based his life on something other than God's grace and mercy and easily came to desire death as soon as that false god was removed. We do not know what ultimately happened to Jonah, but based on how great God's grace was to the wicked Ninevites, I trust God's grace was sufficient for Jonah as well.

PAUL
2 CORINTHIANS 1; PHILIPPIANS 1

Before he came to believe in Christ as the long-awaited Messiah, Paul (then Saul, a well-educated Jewish man) participated in the persecution of the earliest Christian witnesses to Israel. As Paul headed out to take his persecution campaign abroad, Jesus met Paul and opened Paul's eyes to who He really was by temporarily removing Paul's physical sight. After that encounter, Paul's life changed radically. His extensive international travel became focused on bringing people to Christ instead of persecuting them. Paul was committed to his new purpose and knew the remainder of his life was to be entirely devoted to Christ. But that doesn't mean Paul's life became easier or that he became so emotionally detached he was always able to rise above his circumstances. Quite the opposite, in fact—Paul knew suffering and hard times would now be a part of his life, and not only his life but most other Christians' lives as well. As an apostle, Paul knew his job in part was to warn new churches of believers to expect such hard times.

In his second letter to the Corinthians, the now Apostle Paul informed those at Corinth that he did want them to be unaware of the affliction he and his traveling companions had experienced while spreading the gospel in Asia. Paul admitted: "For we were so utterly burdened beyond our strength that we despaired of life itself. Indeed, we felt that we had received the sentence of death." What purpose could God have in giving His missionaries such a burden? Paul explained: "But that was to make us rely not on ourselves but on God who raises the dead. He delivered us from such a deadly peril, and He will deliver us. On Him we have set our hope that He will deliver us again." Why would Paul share this with the new believers in Corinth? What could they do about his burdens, or what can we do? "You also must help us by prayer, so that many will give thanks on our behalf for the blessing granted us through the prayers of many."[128]

Do you ever feel like Paul or know your loved one did? So utterly burdened beyond strength so as to despair of life? Feeling such despair does not mean the person is not a believer. The Apostle Paul despaired of life his burdens were so great, and he is one of the most reputable believers of all time. Most of us, in our flesh, at some time or another become so overwhelmed and heavily burdened we despair of life. This is where believers in Christ should manage expectations for our journeys in this world. Jesus warned us in this world we will have tribulation but to take heart, for He has overcome the world.[129] That's not a maybe, that's a promise. It is a promise that comes with a command to Christians to rely on God when we do have tribulation and despair. Paul discovered the purpose behind tribulation and despair is to force us to realize we cannot rely on ourselves. We have limited strength, willpower and endurance. We are fallible and ultimately this body is weak and destructible. That is exactly why we have to rely on God who is the opposite of all of those earthly limitations. He has unlimited strength and an eternal abode.

The command to rely on God does not only apply to the person who has completed suicide. It is also for us who are left behind, who are despairing the loss of a loved one, to rely on God who raises the dead! Set your hope on Him alone. And while you are waiting to see your hope as reality, pray, as

Paul instructed, so the blessings requested may be granted. Pray for your loved one. Pray knowing God knew beforehand you would pray and may have been moved to save your loved one's soul. Pray for others who are in the midst of despairing burdens now.

As we consider Paul and the blessings granted him through the prayers of many as he requested, it is also important to examine the content of Paul's own prayers. Before Paul became a Christian, he seemed to have a pretty good life. He was a Roman citizen and an extremely well-educated Jewish man. Then he became a Christian and spent a large portion of the rest of his life facing suffering, persecution and imprisonment. I encourage you to scroll through the letters of Paul in the New Testament and observe what is missing from his prayers: noticeably, Paul did not request for his circumstances to change. Paul never asked for the restoration of his comfort and reputation. If I were in prison, I suspect the majority of my prayers would consist of a petition for God to get me out of prison. That may be a very valuable prayer. When I review the prayers of Paul, however, I can see he never prayed for his circumstances to change; he prayed for hearts to change. He asked God for his fellow Christians to not lack in any spiritual gift so they could be sustained in their faith until the return of Jesus.[130] He asked for the peace of God so as the church shared in Christ's sufferings they could also share in His mental comfort.[131] He asked God to give the church the spirit of wisdom to be enlightened and know of its glorious inheritance.[132] And he asked that he may boldly proclaim the gospel, even while in prison.[133]

Finally, I want to give some leeway to my interpretation of this 2 Corinthians passage. What if Paul did not really despair of his life in this situation, but just thought death was inevitable, that he was sure to die by the forces at hand, but was not himself ill content with his life? I would argue the change of interpretation in this passage is not critical, as we can look to nearly any book Paul wrote and see this was not a one-time consideration for Paul.

To him, the result of life or death in his physical body really did not matter. Paul in the flesh had already died; it was no longer Paul who was living but Christ who lived within Paul.[134] That is the truth for every Christian. It is either Jesus by faith (during life on this earth) or Jesus by sight (in death). Paul's ultimate goal was for Christ to be exalted, whether by life or death, and Paul himself said he did not know which option to choose.[135] A lot of people wanted Paul dead for spreading the gospel of Christianity, just as the mobs had wanted Jesus dead before him, and even as Paul himself had wanted Stephen stoned for stirring up trouble with the gospel. Paul could have easily manipulated his circumstances and been put to death by any number of unsavory characters who wanted nothing more than to remove Paul from this world. Paul even admitted he preferred the option of death in his physical body. He knew that to be with Christ in his next life would be much better than his life as a Christian on the earth.[136] Paul knew death would be a preferable result for him.[137]

Despite Paul's desire to depart and be with Christ, he resisted the temptation to flee to his true home with Christ and instead remained for others until his ministry was complete.[138] In his famous "to live is Christ and to die is gain" speech I am referencing, Paul was writing to the Philippians, specifically to those members of the church at Philippi, a city in the Roman province of Macedonia. Paul founded the church in the region during a missionary journey of his, and he decided to resist the call of death because he thought his continued presence in his earthly body was necessary for the Philippians' understanding, progress and joy in the Christian faith. Paul was able to put his concern for the new believers ahead of his own desires. I do not want to imply it is always possible for individuals to remain in desperate situations just for the sake of others. We are not all that strong. I know I certainly am not as self-controlled as Paul. Sometimes even reading his letters is too much for me to handle; I cannot even fathom the intensity of being in his shoes or his prison cell. But the great Apostle Paul was not that strong either. He came to rely not on his own strength, which would fail, but on the strength of Christ, which could sustain Paul until the time was right for him to depart.

As I hope you have seen, many great biblical leaders were not enamored with this life any more than our loved ones were. Neither were they strong enough to endure this life on their own strength. Where they excelled, however, was tapping into the resources and strength of God to carry them through those times.

PART FOUR: FOR THOSE LEFT BEHIND

One reason mental health and depression may not be discussed more openly in the church is because many of us are afraid to admit we do not always know why God allows what He does. There is some merit to recognizing that as created beings, we should not always get to demand an answer from a higher authority. Job's friends kept insisting Job must have committed some great sin to cause his calamity. Job did not believe them, and he was right; a bigger, spiritual battle was being fought that had nothing to do with Job's actions. Although we may not always understand or agree with the reasoning behind God's actions or inaction, the Bible does shed some light on why God allows suffering.

A first step to understanding why is to consider your perspective. For us as created beings, we have an internal longing for immortality but are often focused on what happens in a single life span. Only God can see the bigger picture, can understand the conditions of eternity, and can mold us to make the most of our eternal lives. Indeed, God, knowing we would ask, tells us why we may suffer various trials in this life:

> In this [faith] you rejoice, though now for a little while, if necessary, you have been grieved by various trials, so that the tested genuineness of your faith—more precious than gold that perishes

101

though it is tested by fire—may be found to result in praise and glory and honor at the revelation of Jesus Christ.[139]

The inspired writer of this text, Peter, continued to instruct the recipients of his letter that the outcome of their faith, which itself may be the outcome of our grief, was the very salvation of their souls. This pattern of breaking down to build up is common. When we want to get in better physical shape, we do not consider it odd that we need to work out. Working out is just stress; it is a tearing down of our body so it rebuilds stronger and fitter. When we want our perfect suburban home to have better landscaping, we prune the shrubbery and cut the grass so that it grows back thicker and healthier. These are just modern-day, first world examples that parallel Peter's. During the time of his writing, the readers of his letter would have known Peter was describing the final production stage in gold, which is burning off all impurities to get to a valuable product. A good goldsmith would burn off the bad qualities until the final product was so pure he could see his own reflection. The pure gold can handle the heat from the fire, but the impurities cannot. Fire created something better than the lump the goldsmith held in his hand before the fire. While we are on this earth seeking perfection in a mirror, God has in mind an eternal perfection that necessarily looks more like Him. In the midst of his despair, Job said it best: "But He knows the way that I take; when He has tried me, I shall come out as gold."[140]

In addition to considering God as a human goldsmith, consider God as a true father. Most parents will discipline their kids when they lie, or hit someone, or react poorly to not immediately getting their way. Parents do not do this because they want to; when a child is reacting poorly in a grocery store, I am certain most parents would much rather let their child have whatever they want for immediate peace. Always letting a child have and do what he or she thinks is best is not a good long-term solution. A child has to learn that you will not always get what you want and you cannot let it consume your whole being. Because the parent has a better perspective than the child, the parent has to do the hard things to prepare a child for when he or she does not get what he or she wants out of a relationship, or out of a job, or out of this life. The parent is thinking of the future person, not the child who hates them in the moment. The child in turn suffers for the moment, but in theory also develops in some small way from each disappointment that will shape a better future. Likewise, God knows that what our hearts most long for is an eternal life: ultimate immortality. To save our souls and have an eternity with the only One who will fill the eternity-size hole we feel inside of us, we must learn a faith, a faith that has been tested and tried. Such a faith, says Peter, requires temporary suffering. Our impurities and our irrational demands must be burned away and discarded to make way for something capable of lasting forever.

How much are we adding to our own suffering by adding this layer of questioning and spending so much agony in the "why"? How much time do we spend wondering why God would allow such suffering? How much time do we spend wondering why God would not have prompted us to do just one thing differently? Why God would not have touched our loved one with more compassion? Why God would have given our loved one more than he or she could bear? But why do we spend all of this time wondering why something better did not happen, when we know that we live in a sinful and fallen world? We know God is refining (through fire, because that is the only way to refine) every one of His people so that we look to Him and more like Him. If we really knew why specific incidents of suffering and pain come into our lives, would we ever be able to love or trust God? If we knew all the answers, would we ever be able to grow into a faith worth more than gold? If God is so small to me that He owes me a specific explanation every time an action is taken that I do not agree with, then I have to admit that the one I am praying to is just someone I made up in my own mind to assist me in reaching my own goals. And that somehow this "god" has done something I did not have planned or want done and so now he must explain to me, the master, why he has gone off the course I have created. On the other hand, if God is so big to me that I really believe He could have saved my loved one, that He could even save me, then I have to believe God is majestic enough to have reasons completely inexplicable to me. I must consider He may have a refinement in mind beyond my wildest expectations. He may have a future and an eternity in mind for me and my loved ones that exceeds my wildest dreams. And the path to that eternity may look different than what I envision and plan.

For me, I never struggled as much with this concept as I did after losing someone to suicide. I could see how I could be refined by the loss as a survivor, and how it would test my faith and how it could grow my dependence on God. But what about the person lost to suicide? What about him? How did suffering to the point of death bring him a faith worth more than gold? And worse, what if it did not? I ultimately come back to a question I cannot answer. I do not know what conversations a person may have with God in his or her last minutes. I do not know how the Spirit may show up to walk someone through such pain. I just cannot know. But I have seen it in the Bible. I have seen it in the characters we have discussed here, and I have realized how merciful and gentle God was when His creation did not want to go on living. I have heard the gospel story of how God also suffered to the point of death to make eternal life a possibility for His creation.

I also know, as I trust you do as well, how much absolute evil and heartache there is on this side of heaven, and that reading the Bible changes the questions you ask. The more you realize the Bible guarantees suffering and persecution and tribulation in the present age, the question becomes less of a "Why?" and more of a thanksgiving for the time with our loved ones, a thanksgiving that our loved ones lived for as much and as long as they did, a thanksgiving that there is a hope we will see them again because Jesus bought and paid for all of our sins, up to and including self-inflicted death.

Our entire faith—the essence of the Christian faith—is that the One who did nothing wrong suffered without cause and paid the ultimate price. This is the God we worship, the God who can bring all of humanity, past, present and future, into immortality and out of unjust suffering. Does it not seem odd, then, that we would go through life thinking adherence to the same God would in some way exempt us from suffering? Suffering was the path He walked to salvation for the entire world. The Pharisees, the Romans, Jesus's earthly family—they all had an entire book (in the Old Testament) foretelling Jesus and His suffering. They knew the stories concerning the Messiah very well. But because Jesus's death did not fit the narrative they had created in their own minds, they could not see the glory until after death was defeated; there were no shouts for joy until after Jesus was resurrected. What are you questioning on this side of eternity that will not make sense until you reach the thanksgiving you will know on the other side? Have you, like those in Jesus's time, created a narrative as to what this life should be that you need to surrender to live the life God planned? God's plan guarantees a resurrection and defeat of death; what does your plan guarantee?

It is important to point out that suffering itself does not come from God. God does allow for testing to know (and mold) our hearts, but it is the evil resulting from sin that creates the suffering we experience in this world. Even in the case of Job, God allowed Satan to cause Job's suffering, but it was not at God's hand. God allows us to follow our own free will, which has catastrophic results. But of all the gods out there, our God is the only God who knows the suffering we experience. Our God is the only God who was tested and tried and starved and beaten and ultimately murdered. Our God is the only compassionate God who openly wept at the death of His friend and at the agony faced by surviving friends and family. Our God is the only

God who can truly help us through suffering not because He authored any suffering, but because He experienced much of the same suffering. Jesus knew He was going to die when He went to the cross. He anticipated it. That is a God who knows exactly how to connect with people who know their own death is ahead of them.

The Bible contains many promises and much hope, but many, many more warnings. This realization of the true promises in the Bible really changes the question—I become less surprised by the reality that my brother is gone and more surprised that I am still here. I am more surprised every day that any of us would warrant the new mercies of the morning. The world asks why bad things happen to good people. A dive into the word of God makes you ask why good things happen to all of us bad people.

FOREGOING THE ULTIMATUMS

Another normal stumbling block in the healing process is the ultimatum prayer. You know how it goes: it starts with "Why, God?" and ends with "If you are really God, then you would do [insert whatever you think God should do]." We have some evidence God may ignore such a prayer, as He did when He was dying on the cross between two criminals: "One of the criminals who were hanged railed at Him, saying 'Are you not the Christ? Save yourself and us!'"[141] How did Jesus respond to that? He ignored him completely; He did not even acknowledge the question. And yet see how quick Jesus was to respond to the other criminal, the one who rebuked the thief for demanding to be released from his penalty:

> But the other rebuked him, saying, "Do you not fear God, since you are under the same sentence of condemnation? And we indeed justly, for we are receiving the due reward of our deeds; but this man has done nothing wrong." And he said, "Jesus, remember me when you come into your kingdom." And He said to him, "Truly, I say to you, today you will be with me in paradise."[142]

Both men were criminals, but one was ignored by Christ and the other ushered into paradise with Him. This is a perfect example of how quick Jesus is to forgive and how reluctant we are to ask for that forgiveness. Instead of coming to Christ in humility, human nature is to come to Christ with demands or negotiations. We can bring nothing to Christ except surrender, and it is amazing to see in the stories we have shared of how well surrender works. When we beseech God, He is gracious to us. When we give God an ultimatum, He ignores us in our arrogance. It is hard to understand because it is countercultural: the world has trained us to not let people see weakness. The most successful businessmen are those with the best poker face. Approaching Jesus with nothing is counterintuitive.

I certainly wish I had a greater understanding of why God does what He does and allows what He does, but the truth is that His thoughts are not our thoughts, His ways are not our ways, and as the heavens are higher than the earth, so much higher are His ways and thoughts than ours.[143] The depth of the wisdom and knowledge of God is so great that His judgments are unsearchable and His ways are impossible for us to understand.[144] I have seen a bumper sticker that reads, "God is my copilot." But that is exactly what God refuses to be. God is either the pilot or He's nothing at all. He is either your Lord or He is not truly in your life. He is either doing what you want and you are actually your own god, or He's doing what He ordained before the foundation of the world and you are submitting to that. Such is the case even when what He has ordained or allowed to take place seems unbearable or preposterous or just plain hurtful. That is what a god is— someone who does not have to explain himself to you or respond to your ultimatums.

You know this hierarchy in your own life. For example, if one of my direct reports at work does something I question, that employee must answer to me and explain why I should accept the work. But on the other hand, if my boss does something that does not make any rational or logical sense—and I assure you, such occurs the majority of the time—I still do not get to tell him that if he was really the boss, he would do it my way. If I offered such an ultimatum, I believe he would tell me it could be arranged for him to not be my boss anymore (and so I keep my mouth shut). Such an example seems limp in comparison to asking God why He felt it okay to let your loved one die, but it is the same bowing of the heart in action, the same humility and the same acknowledgment of authority. Jesus came to this earth and called Himself God, upset the structure of temple worship and claimed to heal people. He was a lot of things, but He was not an average guy. He was not just another prophet. Either He was certifiably crazy and needed to be medicated or He was God and does not need to answer to you.

In saying this, however, I do not want you to be afraid to come to God; rather, I want you to consider how you view God in a time of grieving. Hopefully, through the biblical stories shared here you have realized God is much more merciful than man. Jesus was compassionate toward those who approached Him for healing and accepting of their questions and confusion. God responds so long as we realize in our questioning that we still answer to Him, the God of the universe. We cannot threaten or give ultimatums; rather, we surrender, no matter the answer or the outcome. The point of Christianity is that God must be both the means and the end, instead of just a means to an end. When you reach the point when life seems meaningless, and as a reader I believe you are at least acquainted with this feeling, then the substitute god you have worshiped in your heart has died. Fortunately, even at the death of that idol, the actual, real, eternal God has not died. He is there for you, even if He does not always do what you want.

THE UNFORGIVABLE

A friend of mine who lost her adult son to suicide told me her son left a letter explaining why he believed God would forgive him for his last act. The fact that he believed Jesus was his only hope for salvation is all she really needed to know. Once someone has truly had a transformation of the heart to follow Jesus, nothing can be done to take away his or her salvation. Jesus testifies to this truth Himself:

> I give them eternal life, and they will never perish, and no one will snatch them out of my hand. My Father, who has given them to me, is greater than all, and no one is able to snatch them out of the Father's hand.[145]

If you live in the midst of cultural Christianity, you may know of churchgoers or nominal Christians who have come and gone from the "Christian circle." The sad reality is that people who leave the faith were in fact never really of the faith.[146] If a person believes in his heart that Jesus is Lord and God raised Him from the dead, he will be saved, no matter what circle he runs in, where he lives, or what he does.[147] It is a heart change that makes followers of Jesus, not a résumé of dos and do-nots. Our American culture has somehow turned Christianity into a political platform or another stepping stone to appear socially acceptable. If you are a Christian, then you should fit a particular mold created by society. Christians do not have to fit a superficial cultural mold; their focus is on adhering to a biblical mold established by Christ and anchored in His freedom. Not only are Christians not guaranteed social acceptance or ease of life, Christians should be more familiar with being outcast. They encounter sin, trouble and suffering; in fact, in my reading of the Bible, it seems as though Christians should experience these struggles more often than not.

Hopefully you have seen in what you have read here that even the most dedicated, estimable Christians will still stumble in sin of all kinds and, because this world is sinful, Christians will experience suffering while in this world.[148] Fortunately, a Christian's résumé of successes and failures is not what matters. God saves us by His grace and His grace alone. There is nothing we can do, no action we can take or forgo, for salvation is a gift of God.[149] God does not look at your loved one's life and say: "Oh dear! I see suicide in here, and that's not allowed." Do not misunderstand; it is a sin, and all sin grieves God. But suicide is not the one unpardonable sin. We should never be focused on the sin, but rather focused on the only One whose blood is bigger than any sin. It is so easy to look at one act or one sin or one repeated shortcoming and say that thing or specifically that suicide must be more than God can forgive. The problem with such thinking is not realizing how very big God is and how very great was His sacrifice. Yes, our sins are great, but His blood is greater.

In fact, the Bible identifies only one unpardonable sin and that is blasphemy against the Holy Spirit, identified in Mark 3:28–29, Matthew 12:31–32 and Luke 12:10. Hear this truth from the mouth of Jesus:

> Truly, I say to you, all sins will be forgiven the children of man, and whatever blasphemies they utter, but whoever blasphemes against the Holy Spirit never has forgiveness, but is guilty of an eternal sin.[150]

In the context of the gospels where Jesus made this proclamation, Jesus had been performing miracles and casting out demons through the power of the Holy Spirit. The religious leaders of the day, however, refused to accept the power and providence of the Holy Spirit and instead asserted Jesus was using demonic powers. They were denying the power of the Holy Spirit. In today's context, this would be the conscious and continuous rejection of the Holy Spirit, which testifies that Jesus Christ is Lord and Savior. This is the one sin that condemns for eternity: the rejection of the Holy Spirit. On the other hand, if you have accepted Jesus and received the Holy Spirit, the Apostle Paul reassures us, "neither death nor life, nor angels nor rulers, nor things present nor things to come, nor powers, nor height nor depth, nor anything else in all creation"—and all creation includes those persons who fall to suicide—"can separate us from the love of God."[151]

While Jesus was hanging on the cross between the two criminals, one criminal mocked Him and the other asked Jesus for remembrance when He came into His kingdom. Jesus did not say, "It's too late for you!" Not at all. Jesus confirmed the repentant thief on the cross would be with Him in paradise that very day. We see this also in Jesus's parable of the prodigal son who had squandered everything and came crawling back to his father with nothing to offer but shame. The father did not reject his long-lost son and send him away. Instead the father exalted him! That is because with our heavenly father's love, it is not our timing or our actions that matter, it is whether we have trusted that Jesus is greater than all our sin and all our shame, and even all our good deeds and all our wealth. It is running toward our father with nothing in our hands. It is Jesus plus nothing. Jesus plus no actions, Jesus plus no time, Jesus plus nothing. It is also Jesus minus nothing. Neither your blood nor the blood of your loved one is strong enough to negate the power of Jesus's blood. It is a matter of belief and trust in the Savior, regardless of how an individual ultimately leaves this earthly body. No one can ever be good enough to satisfy a holy and perfect God; only Jesus as

God Himself could do that. That sacrifice has been made. Anyone who accepts His sacrifice is stepping into His place of righteousness, just as the thief did on the cross that day. The Apostle Paul informed the Christian church at Thessalonica that he did

> not want you to be uninformed, brethren, about those who are asleep, so that you will not grieve as do the rest who have no hope. For if we believe that Jesus died and rose again, even so God will bring with Him those who have fallen asleep in Jesus.[152]

These verses contain a promise that those who believe Jesus died and rose again will themselves rise again after they die. They also contain a command for those left behind to grieve with hope that those "asleep" in Jesus will live again. The term "asleep" is generally thought to be a euphemism commonly used in the New Testament to refer to those who have died. But what if, instead of considering the word "asleep" to mean "dead" in the contexts it appears in the Bible, we took it at face value? Try thinking of this from God's perspective—to God, no one dies. Human beings go from one state of existence on the earth He created to another state of existence based on the individual's acceptance or rejection of Jesus Christ as the sacrifice for sin. What is dead to God? He sees us in this body; He will see us in our next body. When Jesus said asleep, what if he really meant asleep? What if, once again, our perspective is shortsighted?

Please also note the conditions, or more accurately the lack thereof, to the promises Paul shared with the Thessalonians here: Paul does not say God will bring with Him those who have fallen asleep in Jesus and have not completed suicide or murder of any kind. Paul does not say God will bring with Him those who were perfectly sinless and had perfect church attendance. Paul says God will bring with Him those who have fallen asleep in Jesus, those who have left this earth accepting that Jesus Christ has already paid the price for sin. Do not let man add conditions where God has not. Do not make this harder on yourself or your loved ones than it was designed by the creator.

RECOGNIZE SPIRITUAL BATTLES

If you are reading this and considering suicide in hopes of joining your loved one, do not. No equivocations. Do. Not. These writings, either mine or the Lord's, are not intended to be, neither should they be perceived as, justification for the act of suicide. These writings are intended to be a voice crying out in an area where the church has been at best reluctant to speak and at worst refuses to speak despite the facts that suicide is not only presented in the Bible but is also a public health epidemic among the body of believers that needs to be addressed. It is true that I do not know your circumstances. I do not know what you have been through, what you are going through now or what the future will hold. But I know that things can change. There are so many reasons you may be feeling as you are now. Consider David, a king, a man who killed a giant with a stone, a rich and powerful leader and conqueror who, in Psalm 6, said he was "weary with moaning; every night I flood my bed with tears; I drench my couch with my weeping. My eye wastes away because of grief; it grows weak because of all my foes[153]." This great king, whose heart Christians strive to emulate, was not immune to debilitating grief. Consider another example of desperation from the Old Testament: the Israelites. God rescued the Israelites from enslavement by the powerful Egyptians with supernatural plagues God sent to torment the pharaoh of Egypt until the pharaoh was willing to release the Israelites from slavery. God carried the Israelites through the desert, physically present with them as a cloud during the day and as a fire during the night. God parted great bodies of water just long enough for the Israelites to cross on dry land, but not so long as to allow their enemies to follow. He rained down bread from heaven to keep them alive, and did so every day so they could travel light. Then when the Israelites came to the land of the Amorites the Lord had promised to them, the Israelites paused. They had been told not to fear but they were nevertheless afraid. And when they sent their own kinsmen into the land to spy it out, they saw strong men and fortified walls. In response, the Israelites determined God hated them. After all the miracles they had witnessed firsthand, they asserted God hated them and hated them so much He had spun them through the desert for forty years just so the Amorites could kill them. That would be quite the long con on God's part. But you already know God did not hate the Israelites. You already know God did not give up on them, despite their shortcomings (and no small amount of paranoia). You know this because you are reading this book instead of (though I hope in addition to) the Bible because the Bible is so very long, and the Bible is so very long because God had to finish telling the story of how much He loved the Israelites. God loves them so much He brings them up again in the book of Revelation, at the end of the Bible and the end of the world, detailing how He still makes a way to rescue the Israelites from themselves. The entirety of the Bible is a love story between God and Israel. Similarly, God still loves you and your loved one, just as He loves all who have allowed Jesus to make peace with God for them.

In the midst of any season of desperation, be mindful there may be more to what is going on around you than you realize. Recall that when the authors of the New Testament gospels speak of healing the sick, whether by Jesus or by His disciples, they all add the healing of demon possession to the list of tasks. Jesus healed the sick and cast out demons, then sent the disciples out both to heal disease and to cast out unclean spirits. I am not saying you are, or your loved one was, possessed by a demon; I am saying supernatural forces may be as common as sickness and paralysis. This should not be a surprise to us. In the book of Ephesians, the Apostle Paul told us we do not wrestle against flesh and blood, but against the rulers, authorities, cosmic powers and spiritual forces of evil in the heavenly places.[154] I fear many people lose the physical battle because they fight only with physical weapons, when what is needed—in addition to all of the other tools at our disposal—is spiritual weapons such as the word of God, prayer and proclamation of the gospel.

This concept became very real to me when I visited a tribe in Papua New Guinea. While I was there, I saw members of the tribe attempt to cast out what they perceived as demons inside a woman by covering her and themselves with tree leaves and dancing around her. Imagine a handful of tropical trees dancing around you—would that make you feel better? It resembled a Christmas musical where the trees come alive to sing. I am certain I am not doing justice to the entire ceremony and it undoubtedly followed some prescription to which I was not privy, but as an American I was prone to think: That's so crazy! That is absolutely not going to work! But is it crazier that this particular tribe saw everything as spiritual or crazier that in our Western culture we typically see nothing as spiritual?

We are so tempted to treat mental and physical disorders of all kinds with just medicine, with just doctors, with just the right formula of drugs. Thank the Lord we have access to medicines and doctors and a wealth of knowledge and opportunities. These are wonderful gifts—take advantage of these gifts! Notice, however, that in the New Testament we see the physical and spiritual concerns grouped together, and both had to be addressed. The disciples set out to heal both physical ailments and spiritual ailments, and indeed no one gave more warnings about the devil and his forces of evil than Jesus Himself.

One thing I desperately hope you see in this book is that too many "pleasing" Bible verses are taken out of context, context that is more often than not full of suffering and persecution. Just as plucking those happy verses out of the surrounding circumstances can give a misguided impression of God's word, the same can happen with Jesus's teachings. Jesus gave many warnings about the devil, so let us not be so quick to think demonic supernatural forces are inconceivable or just a product of antiquated times. Even as we believe Jesus when He says we can look to Him for help and guidance, believe His warnings when He tells us the devil is always looking for people to accuse and destroy. Recall the circumstances surrounding Judas's betrayal of Jesus. Biblical text states that before Judas went out to betray Jesus on the night Jesus was ultimately arrested, Satan himself "entered into" Judas.[155] Does that mean Judas was a great guy who was suddenly and instantaneously demon possessed, forever changing the course of history? Not necessarily. Previous texts showed Judas was a thief, loving the things of the world. The Apostle Paul later connects the dots on these details regarding Judas to confirm that when people are following and loving the world, the spirit of evil at work in that disobedience provides an opportunity to further entice a person to carry out the desires of the flesh instead of the will of God.[156] Judas would not have needed a dramatic Hollywood-style exorcism to get rid of the devil; rather, he would have needed to resist his temptation to indulge his flesh and continue in his sin. The Bible commands that when you are angry, do not sin by letting your anger linger—by not letting the sun go down on your anger—and thereby giving an opportunity to the devil.[157] Letting sin linger in your heart gives the opportunity, as it did with Judas, for evil influence to take root. If you are tempted to steal for lack of things you want, the Bible encourages you to labor so that you can own goods to share instead of envying the belongings of others.[158] This is the general anecdote to sin: go the other way. Flee toward the contrary. It was Judas's sin, which he did not resist but instead let grow within him, that gave the devil his opening.

Judas is not the only example in the Bible of evil spirits wreaking havoc on individual lives. Revisit the story of King Saul. He was tormented by an evil spirit and relied on his successor, David, to play music for him so that the evil spirit would temporarily depart.[159] Go even farther back to the story of Job. He was physically ill, scraping his skin with broken pottery, and the root of the problem was that he was under a spiritual attack from Satan. I expect many will read my recounting of events in Papua New Guinea and feel pity for the tribespeople because they do not have access to better resources or do not know any better. I would argue, however, that all cultures, all regions and all education levels tend to have a blind spot to either believing entirely in supernatural forces or not at all. Jesus, on the other hand, as well as His disciples, treated both physical and spiritual ailments. On some occasions, Jesus would state clearly a physical ailment was a result of sin. On other occasions, Jesus would confirm a physical ailment was not a result of sin, but rather an opportunity for the work of God to be displayed. With either illness or condition, rest assured that for those who believe in Christ, there is never any need to fear, as the Spirit of the Lord is stronger than anything else. Greater is God, whose Spirit is in you, than the spirit of the world. Be confident but aware there are many false spirits and false prophets in the world.

To reiterate: I do not want to discourage the use of modern medicine in any way. I do want to encourage those who have not found relief in the world's solutions to assess whether they are evaluating the entire human being. Human beings are extremely complex, and issues may be physical, emotional, spiritual or a combination of the three. If you just go to a psychiatrist, the psychiatrist may assert your problem is a chemical imbalance in your brain that requires medicine and treatment. If you just go to a medical doctor, the medical doctor may assert your problem is a hormonal imbalance, perhaps something wrong with the thyroid that (after multiple additional costly scans) will require a different medicine and additional treatment. If you just go to a pastor, the pastor may assert your problem is entirely spiritual and prayer and fasting are needed. But human beings are so intricate and multifaceted! We are so privileged to have so many experts of all different specialties that each expert has usually learned to focus on his or her area of expertise to the neglect of all others. That is not a bad thing when you are becoming an expert, but when you are a human being in distress, you may need to use all of the tools at your disposal to finally get the help you need. A line, often attributed to C. S. Lewis, of George MacDonald's says: "You do not have a soul. You are a soul. You have a body." Our bodies will change. We see that on this earth, and we see in the Bible that one day we will have resurrected bodies that are not subject to decay.[160] The soul will still be the soul, you will still be you and our loved ones in Jesus will be together with our earthly scars. Be open to the entirety of the soul now in case it needs attention a prescription alone cannot treat.

REASSESS CHOOSING DEATH OVER LIFE

I have discovered that many people cannot comprehend the depression and fear that lead to suicide, but seem perfectly able to understand (and show more compassion to) those on the opposite end of the spectrum who have a death grip on their own lives. I am sure you know of someone like this; in fact, it may be everyone you know. Such people are afraid of death, they are afraid of change and they idolize this life and this body God has given us. Such a life choice is as extreme as suicide. A person making that choice is not living and is not experiencing the freedom that comes from looking forward to an eternal life.

I would imagine there is a middle ground between the two extremes based on the seemingly simplistic solution to surrender this life to living for God. As pat and easy as that may sound, I fully appreciate that it is not. Knowing God and letting God be in control of the number of your days, and even how those days are spent, is incredibly difficult. (Or at least so I have heard, as I still am not able to do it.) No matter how difficult it is for you to face the day or even the minute ahead, and no matter how long and arduous it seems, your life and the tasks you face are actually going to be quite short in the scheme of things. You are but a mist.[161]

In this day and age, we have the benefit of having a lot of history behind us; a lot of great people and times and empires have already come and gone. We can look at that from the perspective of our own workweek or school day or even one more minute inside of our own minds and realize our life span in this body is going to be very short. That does not necessarily make it any easier. I do not want to encourage you to just "get through it" or just "bear with it." I want to encourage you to surrender to the only God who can use all of your struggles for your own good. God has made a promise to use all of life's difficulties for good for those who trust in Him, and I for one do not want all these hardships to be wasted.[162]

Sometimes people left behind after a death can identify with those who completed suicide and have a glimpse of the anguish and pain that is strong enough to convince a person he or she has no other choice. Sometimes survivors grapple to comprehend what could lead to someone taking their own life. Which is crazier? That some of us clutch onto our brief existence, or that some of us are compelled to hasten the inevitable? If both are sinful, why does the church so often focus its chastisement on the latter instead of the former? Ultimately, we should give God control over these decisions, but in either case, we should also be focusing our hope during life with our future dwelling in view. In discussing some of the Old Testament faithful, such as Abraham and Sarah, Enoch and Abel, the writer of Hebrews notes they:

> acknowledge that they were strangers and exiles on the earth. For people who speak thus make it clear they are seeking a homeland. If they had been thinking of that land from which they had gone out, they would have had opportunity to return. But as it is, they desire a better country, that is, a heavenly one. Therefore God is not ashamed to be called their God, for He has prepared for them a city.[163]

If we as Christians are all living as exiles after the example of the faithful gone before us, it may make more sense for us to be longing to leave this world in much the same way Paul and other faithful servants were. Shouldn't it conceivably be more socially acceptable in Christian circles to be filled with anxiety to leave a broken world for an eternal one? Has Christian culture placed so much value on this temporary life that we have lost perspective?

Regardless of which view is crazier, faith and faith alone, not our sins, determines our eternal city. Taking a life in this world is temporary, but the suicide of rejecting Jesus Christ is permanent. For where there is forgiveness of our sins through the blood of Jesus, God has promised to forget our lawless deeds. God has said there is no longer any need for sacrifice or payment for our sins because He does not even remember the sins we have committed against Him.[164] That is true for the sins we commit every day, and that is true for the sins our loved ones commit in a moment or season of suffering and weakness. Nothing we can do can change who God is and what God has said, for even if we are faithless, He will remain faithful.[165]

KNOW SOMEONE IS FIGHTING FOR YOU

In several places in the Bible, we see the throne of God may at times resemble a courtroom. We see this at the beginning of Job, where Satan accused Job before God. We also see this in Zechariah chapter three, in which the prophet Zechariah had a vision involving Joshua, a high priest for the Israelites who had returned to Israel after being exiled in Babylon. In his vision, Zechariah saw both Joshua and Satan standing before God, with Satan there to accuse Joshua. In that particular courtroom drama, Joshua, as Israel's high priest, was likely representing the entire people of Israel who were being accused by Satan before God. Satan apparently accuses everyone before God—even the righteous and upright and God's own chosen nation. In response to Satan's accusations, the angel of the Lord, a pre-incarnate vision of Jesus Christ, took away Joshua's filthy clothes and clothed him with clean clothes. That is what we need to experience as well, and that is what is happening in heavenly courtrooms for those who ask Jesus to remove their filthy clothes and replace them with His own. Jesus is more than willing to give us new clothes and more than willing to argue on our behalf against Satan's accusations. We all need Jesus Christ there in God's courtroom as our constant advocate because we are continually being accused by Satan, and only Jesus can put forth a valid defense for us.[166] Our culture wants us to believe we can present our own argument and provide a valid defense before God, but that is our arrogance blinding us to our own inadequacies. Given the spiritual courtroom, it is to be expected for us to feel guilt and shame. We may replay our sins in our head and then argue our own excuses in defense. A real enemy is constantly accusing us before God, and somehow we know that. We can feel it. We must fight back against him, reminding him and ourselves someone has been convicted of our crimes, someone has paid the price for our crimes, and the personal case against us has to be dismissed. Jesus Christ, as our advocate, is there to remind us and Satan that He has paid for our crimes and that to punish us for our sins would be double jeopardy—a concept any defense attorney (even the ones advertising on highway billboards) can use to get a case thrown out. Remember that in the spiritual case you are fighting, someone is fighting for you and your loved one.[167] Remember that your loved one may have very well had the best defense attorney money cannot even buy.

KNOW WE ARE ALL HERE

When Paul and Silas were jailed in Philippi for spreading the gospel of Jesus Christ, they were praying and singing hymns within their jail cell when a great earthquake came and loosened the jailers' chains and opened up all the prison doors. This story in Acts chapter sixteen tells us that when the prison guard saw the prison doors were open, he immediately drew his sword and was about to kill himself when Paul cried out with a loud voice, saying, "Do not harm yourself, for we are all here!"[168] The prison guard knew he would be humiliated and ultimately executed by the authorities if any prisoners escaped. He was going to spare himself the agony of waiting for the inevitable from the hands of his supervisors.

I tell you the same thing now: Do not harm yourself, for we are all here. Yes, death is inevitable for all of us. Yes, there may be no small amount of humiliation and agony along the way. But we are all here. Jesus Christ is here for you, without question. The church is here for you, though sometimes that is hard to see when the church is filled with human beings also struggling with sin and the flesh. But we are all here, trying to figure it out also. We are all here, living through our own shame-filled and sin-ridden pasts. We are all here, with our doubts and insecurities. We are all here, uncertain as to what the future will hold or when death will come. We are all here, mourning our loved ones and wondering what we could have possibly done to rewrite the ending. Please stay here with us.

KNOW THIS IS NOT THE END

Ultimately, all things work together for good for those who love Him. That is not a promise for this life, and in fact, everything may not work out well in this life. The promise is for eternity, which is so much more important than this life. The promise is not reserved for those who die of natural causes, but is for all who have loved Jesus and believed in Him. When Adam and Eve sinned in the Garden of Eden, they prevented any chance of this earth being our eternal home. We are all dying here in one way or another. The flesh may be tired and weary and depressed and want to leave this world. But in the words of Paul, put on the Lord Jesus Christ and make no provision for the flesh to gratify its desires.[169] The ability to do so, the ability to make that choice, is in many ways still an avenue for the workings of the grace of God. We know from the book of Revelation, for example, that in the end of days people will be in such torment that they will long to die and be unable to even complete the act of suicide. For now, we must continue to struggle against the flesh.

Farming and gardening parables are used in many places in the Bible, and so I will end with one here: a plant's seed is not dying when it goes underground; it is getting ready to spring to life. I hope that in death, our loved ones found true and eternal life beyond their wildest hopes and have sprung to life even as you read this. Job suffered long before Jesus came to make eternal life with God possible, but Job knew God already had a plan for salvation. Job asserted he may wait for deliverance all of his days, but that even in death God would call and Job would be able to answer.[170] I pray with all of my heart, for your loved one and mine, that God answered. Since the beginning of time, all mankind has rebelled against God. Some of those rebels were still heaven bound.

REFERENCES

[1] @JarridWilson. "Loving Jesus doesn't always cure suicidal thoughts. Loving Jesus doesn't always cure depression. Loving Jesus doesn't always cure PTSD. Loving Jesus doesn't always cure anxiety. But that doesn't mean Jesus doesn't offer us companionship and comfort. He ALWAYS does that." Twitter, September 9, 2019, 5:01 pm, https://twitter.com/JarridWilson/status/1171166658829803520.

[2] @JarridWilson. "Officiating a funeral for a Jesus-loving woman who took her own life today. Your prayers are greatly appreciated for the family." Twitter, September 9, 2019, 2:01 pm, https://twitter.com/JarridWilson/status/1171121544161976320.

[3] @KayWarren1. "Praying, Jarrid. Her devastated family needs so much tenderness and compassion right now. Grateful for your willingness to be the arms of Jesus to them." Twitter, September 9, 2019, 2:16 pm, https://twitter.com/KayWarren1/status/1171125339302445056.

[4] English Standard Version, John 15:19, 17:16.

[5] Hebrews 13:8.

[6] Laurie, Greg. "Greg's Blog: Jarrid Wilson in Memoriam." Harvest.org, September 10, 2019, https://harvest.org/resources/gregs-blog/post/jarrid-wilson-in-memoriam/.

[7] Wilson, Jarrid. "Why Suicide Doesn't Always Lead to Hell." Jarridwilson.com, June 9, 2018, jarridwilson.com/why-suicide-doesn't-always-lead-to-hell/.

[8] Anthem of Hope. "Christian Mental Health Statistics." Anthemofhope.org, September 5, 2019, http://anthemofhope.org/blog/2019/9/5/christian-mental-health-statistics.

[9] Ibid.

[10] 1 Corinthians 12:12; Romans 12:5.

[11] Czeisler, Mark É., Lane, Rashon I., Petrosky, Emiko, et al. Mental Health, Substance Use, and Suicidal Ideation during the COVID-19 Pandemic—United States, June 24–30, 2020. Morbidity and Mortality Weekly Report 69:1049–1057.

[12] Ibid.

[13] Genesis 4:7.
[14] 2 Samuel 24:14.
[15] Psalm 51:4.
[16] 1 John 3:20.
[17] 2 Timothy 3:16.
[18] Judges 8:33–35.
[19] Judges 9:4.
[20] Judges 9:5.
[21] Judges 9:54.
[22] Psalm 3:3.
[23] Psalm 18:2.
[24] Psalm 28:7.
[25] Psalm 33:20.
[26] Psalm 84:11.
[27] Psalm 89:18.
[28] Psalm 115:9.
[29] 2 Samuel 14:14.
[30] Judges 16:30.
[31] Hebrews 11:32–34.
[32] 1 Samuel 8:7.
[33] 1 Samuel 8:19–20.
[34] 1 Samuel 9:20.
[35] 1 Samuel 9:21.
[36] 1 Samuel 10:24.
[37] 1 Samuel 12:14–15.
[38] 1 Samuel 13:5.
[39] Daniel 10; 2 Kings 6:17–20.
[40] 1 Samuel 13:13–14.
[41] 1 Samuel 15:2–3.
[42] 1 Samuel 15:8–9.
[43] 1 Samuel 15:22.
[44] 1 Samuel 15:23.
[45] 1 Samuel 16; 1 Samuel 18.
[46] 1 Samuel 18.
[47] 1 Samuel 24; 1 Samuel 26
[48] See Romans 1:24.
[49] Deuteronomy 18:11; Leviticus 20:6.
[50] MacArthur, John. The MacArthur Study Bible: New American Standard Bible. Thomas Nelson Bibles, 2014, 413OTn. 28:15.
[51] 1 Samuel 28:19.
[52] Romans 10:9.
[53] John 10:28–30; Romans 8:38–39; Ephesians 4:30; Jude 24.
[54] Luke 16:19–31.
[55] Rigney, Joe. (2015, April 4). "He Descended into Hell?" Retrieved from www.desiringgod.org/articles/he-descended-into-hell.
[56] Revelation 19:9.
[57] 1 Samuel 16:7.

[58] 1 Samuel 10:9–13.
[59] 2 Kings 23:29; 2 Chronicles 35:20-27.
[60] 2 Chronicles 18:33–34.
[61] 1 Samuel 18:7.
[62] 2 Samuel 1:6.
[63] MacArthur, MacArthur Study Bible, 419OTn. 1:10.
[64] 1 Chronicles 10:14.
[65] 1 Chronicles 10:13–14.
[66] Job 14:5.
[67] Psalm 139:16.
[68] 1 Samuel 31:4.
[69] 1 Samuel 16:18.
[70] 1 Samuel 14:7.
[71] 2 Samuel 23:34; 2 Samuel 11:3.
[72] 2 Samuel 15:31.
[73] 2 Samuel 16:21.
[74] 2 Samuel 17:23.
[75] Exodus 20:3.
[76] 1 Kings 16:18.
[77] 1 Kings 16:19.
[78] 1 Kings 11:28.
[79] 1 Kings 14:7–11.
[80] Matthew 10:1.
[81] Matthew 10:8.
[82] Matthew 10:13.
[83] Matthew 26:22.
[84] Romans 3:23.
[85] John 13:27.
[86] James 2:10.
[87] Acts 7:20.
[88] Exodus 2:11.
[89] Acts 7:23.
[90] Luke 19:10.
[91] 2 Samuel 12:14.
[92] 2 Samuel 12:13.
[93] Romans 3:23.
[94] Leviticus 17:11; 2 Corinthians 5:21.
[95] Philippians 3:5–6.
[96] Acts 22:20.
[97] Acts 8:3.
[98] Acts 9:15.
[99] 1 Samuel 16:7.
[100] Romans 4:21–25; 2 Corinthians 5:21.
[101] Deuteronomy 6:6.
[102] Proverbs 4:23.
[103] Mark 5:21–22.
[104] Numbers 11:14.

[105] Lamentations 3:22–23; Matthew 6:11.

[106] This partner was a great mentor and boss, not to mention extremely beautiful, but bore no similarities to Job.

[107] Job 1:1.

[108] 1 Peter 5:8; John 10:10.

[109] Job 3.

[110] Job 6:4.

[111] Job 6:8–9.

[112] Job 14:1.

[113] Jeremiah 17:9.

[114] John 11:35.

[115] Luke 22:44.

[116] James 5:17.

[117] 1 Kings 17:22.

[118] 1 Kings 19:4.

[119] Philippians 4:19.

[120] Jeremiah 20:7–18.

[121] Lamentations 3:2.

[122] Lamentations 3:6.

[123] Lamentations 3:7, 11, 17.

[124] Lamentations 3:19–24.

[125] Psalm 30:5.

[126] 2 Kings 14:25.

[127] 2 Chronicles 19:7.

[128] 2 Corinthians 1:8–11.

[129] John 16:33.

[130] 1 Corinthians 1:7–9.

[131] 2 Corinthians 1:4–6.

[132] Ephesians 1:17–18.

[133] Ephesians 6:19–20.

[134] Galatians 2:20.

[135] Philippians 1:20–22.

[136] Philippians 1:23.

[137] Philippians 1:21.

[138] Philippians 1:23–24; 2 Corinthians 5:8.

[139] 1 Peter 1:6–7.

[140] Job 23:10.

[141] Luke 23:39.

[142] Luke 23:40–43.

[143] Isaiah 55:8–9.

[144] Romans 11:33.

[145] John 10:28–29.

[146] 1 John 2:19.

[147] Romans 10:9.

[148] Matthew 26:36—46; Romans 7:15–20.

[149] Ephesians 2:4–8.

[150] Mark 3:28–29.

[151] Romans 8:38–39.
[152] 1 Thessalonians 4:13–14.
[153] Psalm 6:6–7.
[154] Ephesians 6:12.
[155] Luke 22:3; John 13:27.
[156] Ephesians 2:1–3.
[157] Ephesians 4:26–27.
[158] Ephesians 4:28.
[159] 1 Samuel 16:15–23.
[160] 1 Corinthians 15:35–58.
[161] James 4:14.
[162] Romans 8:28.
[163] Hebrews 11:13–16.
[164] Hebrews 10:17–18.
[165] 2 Timothy 2:13.
[166] 1 John 2:1.
[167] 2 Kings 6:17–20; Daniel 10.
[168] Acts 16:27–28.
[169] Romans 13:14.
[170] Job 14:14–15.

Printed in Great Britain
by Amazon

11525714R00082